LICENSE AGREEMENT FOR The IIA's CIA LEARNING SYSTEM®

STUDENT MATERIALS

By opening and using The IIA's CIA LEARNING SYSTEM student materials (the "Materials"), the user ("User") hereby agrees as follows:

(i) That The Institute of Internal Auditors is the exclusive copyright owner of the Materials.

(ii) Provided that the required fee for use of the Materials by User has been paid to The IIA or its agent, User has the right, by this License, to use the Materials solely for his/her own educational use.

(iii) User has no right to print or make any copies, in any media, of the materials, or to sell, or sublicense, loan, or otherwise convey or distribute these materials or any copies thereof in any media.

The IIA's CIA Learning System®

The IIA's CIA Learning System® is based on the Certified Internal Auditor® (CIA®) exam syllabus developed by The IIA. Please note that the program developers and subject matter experts do not have access to CIA exam questions. The Learning System does not "teach the test." There may be some content in the Learning System not covered by the certification exams, and, conversely, there may be content tested in the exams that is not covered in the Learning System. While the Learning System is a good tool for study, reading the text and completing the quiz/test questions do not guarantee a passing score on the CIA exam.

Every effort has been made to ensure that all information is current and correct. As laws and regulations change, these materials are not intended to offer legal or professional services or advice. This material is consistent with the revised *Standards* of the International Professional Practices Framework (IPPF) introduced in July 2015, effective in 2017.

Copyright

Acknowledgments

The IIA acknowledges the contributions of its volunteer leaders who shared their time, experience, and insights during the development of The IIA's CIA Learning System.

Subject matter experts

Farah George Araj, CPA, CIA, CFE, QIAL, Australia

Scott Blankenship, CIA, CRMA, CPA, CFE, United States

Melissa Clawson, CIA, CRMA, United States

Christy Decker-Weber, CIA, CRMA, CPA, CFE, CHIAP

Jayson Walter Kwasnik, CIA, CPA, CA, Canada

Jessica Minshew, CIA, United States

Joanne F. Prakapas, CIA, CRMA, CFE, CPA, CFF, United States

James M. Reinhard, CIA, United States

Elizabeth Sandwith, CFIIA, United Kingdom

Past subject matter experts

Pat Adams, CIA

Terry Bingham, CIA, CISA, CCSA

Raven Catlin, CIA, CPA, CFSA

Patrick Copeland, CIA, CRMA, CISA, CPA

Don Espersen, CIA

Michael J. Fucilli, CIA, QIAL, CRMA, CGAP, CFE

James D. Hallinan, CIA, CPA, CFSA, CBA

Larry Hubbard, CIA, CCSA, CPA, CISA

Jim Key, CIA

David Mancina, CIA, CPA

Al Marcella, PhD, CISA, CCSA

Markus Mayer, CIA

Vicki A. McIntyre, CIA, CFSA, CRMA, CPA

Gary Mitten, CIA, CCSA

Lynn Morley, CIA, CGA

Lyndon Remias, CIA

James Roth, PhD, CIA, CCSA

Brad Schwieger, CPA, DBA

Doug Ziegenfuss, PhD, CIA, CCSA, CPA, CMA, CFE, CISA, CGFM, CR.FA., CIT

Part 2: Practice of Internal Auditing

Table of Contents

Part 2: Practice of Internal Auditing

Part 2 of The IIA's CIA Learning System focuses on the auditor's abilities related to the Performance Standards (series 2000, 2200, 2300, 2400, 2500, and 2600). Performance Standards describe the nature of internal auditing and provide quality criteria against which the performance of internal auditing services can be measured. Note that Standard 2100 ("Nature of Work") is addressed in Part 1, Section V, "Governance, Risk Management, and Control."

Part 2 is made up of four sections:

- **Section I: Managing the Internal Audit Activity**. The chief audit executive (CAE) must effectively manage the internal audit activity to ensure that it adds value to the organization (Standard 2000).

- **Section II: Planning the Engagement**. Internal auditors must develop and document a plan for each engagement, including the engagement's objectives, scope, timing, and resource allocations. The plan must consider the organization's strategies, objectives, and risks relevant to the engagement (Standard 2200).

- **Section III: Performing the Engagement**. Internal auditors must identify, analyze, evaluate, and document sufficient information to achieve the engagement's objectives (Standard 2300).

- **Section IV: Communicating Engagement Results and Monitoring Progress**. Internal auditors must communicate the results of engagements (Standard 2400). The CAE must establish and maintain a system to monitor the disposition of results communicated to management (Standard 2500), discuss any remaining unacceptable risk levels with senior management, and communicate any unresolved issues related to unacceptable risk levels to the board (Standard 2600).

Those managing engagements must ensure that the engagements are conducted in a professional manner—from planning through supervision and communication to monitoring engagement outcomes—and with a continuous awareness of risk.

Section I: Managing the Internal Audit Activity

This section is designed to help you:
- Describe policies and procedures of internal auditing operations.
- Interpret administrative activities of internal audit.
- Identify sources of potential engagements.
- Identify a risk management framework to assess risks.
- Prioritize audit engagements based on the results of a risk assessment.
- Interpret the types of assurance engagements.
- Interpret the types of consulting engagements.
- Describe coordination of internal audit efforts with external auditors, regulatory oversight bodies, and other internal assurance functions.
- Describe potential reliance on other assurance providers.
- Describe how the chief audit executive (CAE) communicates the annual audit plan and its results to senior management and the board.
- Identify how the CAE seeks board approval of the annual audit plan.
- Identify significant risk exposures and control and governance issues for the CAE to report to the board.
- Recognize that the CAE reports on the overall effectiveness of the organization's internal control and risk management processes to senior management and the board.
- Identify internal audit key performance indicators that the CAE communicates to senior management and the board periodically.

The IIA's guidance referenced in the Learning System may be accessed using the links below. Access to specific pages and documents varies for the public and The IIA members.
- **Attribute Standards:** www.theiia.org/Attribute-standards
- **Performance Standards:** www.theiia.org/Performance-standards
- **Standards and Guidance:** www.theiia.org/Guidance
- **Position Papers:** www.theiia.org/Position-papers
- **Implementation Guidance:** www.theiia.org/Practiceadvisories
- **Practice Guides and GTAGs:** www.theiia.org/Practiceguides

This section focuses on the criteria for effectively managing the internal audit function at both strategic and operational levels.

Chapter 1: Internal Audit Operations

The internal audit activity plays a critical role in ensuring that the organization's resources are being used efficiently and effectively toward accomplishing organizational objectives and that the organization's internal control framework is adequate for controlling the variety of internal and external risks to which the organization may be vulnerable.

The topics in this chapter focus on the role of internal audit at an operational level, including how the CAE ensures that the activity can fulfill its role and responsibilities. This includes:

- Formulating policies and procedures that support the activity's independence, objectivity, proficiency, and due professional care.
- Directing administrative functions that allow the internal audit activity to operate efficiently and effectively.

Topic A: Internal Audit Policies and Procedures

This topic discusses policies and procedures required to plan, organize, direct, and monitor internal audit operations, including requirements surrounding review and communication of established policies and procedures.

In addition to reviewing the contents of this topic, students can review the following IIA materials:
- Implementation Guidance for Standard 2040

Managing the Internal Audit Activity

Performance Standard 2000, "Managing the Internal Audit Activity," states that the chief audit executive must effectively manage the internal audit activity to ensure that it adds value to the organization. Interpretation tells us that "*the internal audit activity adds value to the organization and its stakeholders when it considers strategies, objectives, and risks; strives to offer ways to enhance governance, risk management and control processes; and objectively provides relevant assurance.*"

From a strategic perspective, the CAE must ensure the establishment of a risk-based plan for managing the internal audit function's activity. This will require that internal audit leaders:

- Manage internal audit changes needed to implement and support the organization's strategy.
- Establish relationships throughout the organization to foster communication and cooperation.
- Assess and promote an ethical climate and good governance.
- Develop an appropriate system to measure the efficiency and effectiveness of the internal audit function and report performance to senior management and the board.
- Manage interactions with external auditors, regulatory bodies, and other internal assurance functions.

From an operational perspective, the CAE must ensure that the function is managed in a professional manner and that:

- Policies and procedures are in place to plan, organize, direct, and monitor internal audit operations.
- The function is administered to make the best use of internal audit resources.
- The function is staffed appropriately for its tasks.
- A risk-based audit plan is used to identify potential engagements and prioritize engagements.
- Senior management is informed about the effectiveness of the organization's internal control and risk management frameworks.
- The quality of internal audit work is monitored, assessed, and reported to senior management, and a quality assurance and improvement program is in place.

Policies and Procedures

Performance Standard 2040, "Policies and Procedures"

The chief audit executive must establish policies and procedures to guide the internal audit activity.

The form and content of policies and procedures are dependent upon the size and structure of the internal audit activity and the complexity of its work:

- Large, mature internal audit activities may have a formal internal audit operations manual that includes policies and procedures.
- Smaller or less mature activities may not have a formal manual and instead may publish policies and procedures as separate documents or as part of an audit management software program.

In addition to policies and procedures, the internal audit manual (or other documentation method) may include information on the quality assurance and improvement program and other administrative matters.

Policies and procedures are one type of tool the CAE has to ensure that internal audit follows a systematic and disciplined approach. They can help everyone involved in the internal audit activity to consistently deliver high-quality service. They are important to ensure that internal audit is meeting the expectations laid out by the *Standards* and senior management.

Policies and procedures should be reviewed periodically, and changes may be communicated:

- In writing.
- During internal audit staff meetings.
- Through training.

When reviewing policies and procedures, the CAE should also consider whether existing policies and procedures, including the internal audit charter, accurately reflect the Core Principles, the Code of Ethics, and the *Standards*.

Documentation of policies and procedures and evidence that they have been clearly communicated to internal audit personnel may be used to demonstrate conformance with Standard 2040.

Policies

Examples of internal audit policies may include:
- The overall purpose and responsibilities of the internal audit activity.
- Adherence to the mandatory guidance of the International Professional Practices Framework (IPPF).
- Independence and objectivity.
- Ethics.
- Protecting confidential information.
- Record retention.

Procedures

Examples of internal audit procedures may include:
- Preparing a risk-based audit plan.
- Planning an audit and preparing the engagement work program.
- Performing audit engagements.
- Documenting audit engagements.
- Communicating results/reporting.
- Monitoring and follow-up process.

Topic B: Internal Audit Administration

This topic discusses the importance of the various administrative activities that must be conducted to support the internal audit activity, including the various resource constraints that must be considered when budgeting for an audit plan.

In addition to reviewing the contents of this topic, students can review the following IIA materials:
- Implementation Guidance for Standard 2030

Administrative Activities

Performance Standard 2030, "Resource Management"

The chief audit executive must ensure that internal audit resources are appropriate, sufficient, and effectively deployed to achieve the approved plan.

The Implementation Guidance for Standard 2030 recommends that the CAE usually begin by gaining a deeper understanding of the resources available to the internal audit activity in the board-approved internal audit plan. This may include:

- The number of internal audit staff.
- The number of productive work hours available. (Productive work hours excludes factors such as paid time off, time spent on training, and administrative tasks.)
- The internal audit activity's collective knowledge, skills, and other competencies. (This information may be found in a documented skills assessment, employees' performance appraisals, and post-audit or regularly scheduled surveys.)
- Approved budget and funds available for training, technology, or additional staffing.

Identified gaps in the quality or quantity of available resources should be addressed by the CAE. This can be accomplished by:

- Providing training for existing staff.
- Hiring additional staff.
- Hiring an external service provider.
- Cosourcing or outsourcing engagements.
- Using one or more guest auditors, for example, an expert from within the organization.
- Developing a rotational audit plan.

Rotational plans can use both inbound and outbound rotation.

- Inbound rotation involves filling certain internal audit job positions with employees from the business for a limited period of time.
- Outbound rotation involves moving internal auditors into business job positions either permanently or for a limited time period, usually between six and 24 months.

Rotational plans can be used to train middle-level management and executives, to train other members of the business, and to bring specialized skills to the internal audit team. Note that a program using guest internal auditors may be similar to a rotation program, except the duration of guest auditor involvement is generally for a shorter term.

It is important that the skill sets of the existing internal audit resources do not become a constraint in how internal audit addresses the risks of the organization.

As part of resource management, it is recommended that the CAE establish a program for selecting and developing the human resources for the internal audit activity.

For the internally staffed portion of the audit group, this program should include:

- Developing written job descriptions for each level of audit staff.
- Selecting qualified and competent individuals.
- Training and providing continuing educational opportunities for each auditor.
- Appraising each internal auditor's performance at least annually.
- Providing counsel to internal auditors on their performance and professional development.
- Considering succession planning for management of internal auditing.

For the externally sourced portion of the audit group, the program should include:

- Selecting qualified and competent individuals aligned to the overall risks and resource needs.
- Reflecting on the provider's performance.
- Developing expectations that sustain strengths, proactively address areas for improvement, and help ensure service excellence.

Across all elements of the internal audit activity, including sourcing of resources, the CAE should define the skill set needs based on:

- The organization's risks.
- The internal audit plan.
- Value drivers of key stakeholders.

The CAE's role in coordination of assurance work is rapidly evolving with increased demands across the organization. Many CAEs are taking a more systematic approach to assurance across the organization because of:

- Increased demands from the organization, board, and senior management.
- The assurance fatigue that may impact line managers when dealing with uncoordinated assurance processes.

CAEs may embrace this systematic approach when generating a schedule for internal audit engagements.

In order to develop a schedule for internal audit engagements as part of the internal audit plan, the CAE must consider:

- The organization's schedule.
- The schedule of individual internal auditors.
- The availability of auditable entities.

By paying attention to the organization's schedule and the availability of auditable entities, internal audit may be able to schedule audits during less-busy times of the year for business units and the organization as a whole. This may help avoid assurance fatigue and promote stronger cooperation efforts from the entities that are being audited.

Chapter 2: Risk-Based Internal Audit Plan

Because internal auditors are experts in understanding organizational risks and internal controls available to mitigate these risks, they are in a unique position to help management protect their organizations from risk exposures—present and future—ranging from minor disruptions to major catastrophes. The internal audit activity assists both management and the oversight body (the board or its audit committee) in enterprise risk management (ERM) by:

- Helping management to understand governance, internal control, and risk management processes.
- Developing and implementing a risk assessment framework for internal audit planning.
- Bringing a systematic, disciplined auditing approach to assessing the effectiveness of internal controls and risk management processes.
- Providing objective and independent assurance that the organization's risks have been appropriately mitigated.
- Making recommendations for improvements as warranted.

Risk is a part of conducting business. Organizations must take risks to pursue their strategies and objectives. The key is to do this while also mitigating or reducing risk.

While helping an organization embrace internal control and ERM frameworks is critical for organizational governance and integral to most controls, internal auditing itself needs to incorporate the same ERM techniques into its audit planning procedures.

To be truly value-added to the organization, the annual audit plan and specific engagements must focus on significant risks. What is considered significant can be defined as those risks that are considered likely (highly probable) and/or those that would have a real impact (highly damaging even if less probable) on the achievement of the organization's objectives or goals for that area.

Topic A: Potential Engagement Sources

Potential engagements may originate from multiple different sources. This topic discusses how the chief audit executive should go about examining and prioritizing the potential engagements.

In addition to reviewing the contents of this topic, students can review the following IIA materials:
- Implementation Guidance for Standard 2010
- Practice Guide, "Developing a Risk-based Internal Audit Plan"

Planning

Performance Standard 2010, "Planning"

The chief audit executive must establish a risk-based plan to determine the priorities of the internal audit activity, consistent with the organization's goals.

Planning is done by the CAE working with senior management and the board to understand:
- Organizational strategies.
- Key business objectives.
- Associated risks.
- Risk management processes.

Implementation Standard 2010.A1 (Assurance Engagements)

The internal audit activity's plan of engagements must be based on a documented risk assessment, undertaken at least annually. The input of senior management and the board must be considered in this process

The internal audit activity typically reviews and corroborates the key risks that were identified by senior management.
- As Standard 2010.A1 indicates, this process must be undertaken *at least* annually.
- In some sectors, annually may not be frequently enough, requiring documented risk assessments to take place much more frequently, such as every quarter.
- Risks are measured in terms of impact and likelihood.

Implementation Standard 2010.A2 (Assurance Engagements)

The chief audit executive must identify and consider the expectations of senior management, the board, and other stakeholders for internal audit opinions and conclusions.

The internal audit plan is developed using:
- The expectations and requests of senior management, the board, and other stakeholders.
- The internal audit activity's ability to rely on the work of other internal and external assurance providers.

This also applies to individual engagement opinions or ratings, as it is important that the CAE and key stakeholders are aligned on expectations of the level of assurance provided by the internal audit.

Implementation Standard 2010.C1 (Consulting Engagements)

The chief audit executive should consider accepting proposed consulting engagements based on the engagement's potential to improve management of risks, add value, and improve the organization's operations. Accepted engagements must be included in the plan.

Both internal and external risks must be examined and linked to specific objectives and business processes to organize and prioritize the risks.

- Internal risks may affect key products and services, personnel, and systems.
  - Relevant risk factors include the degree of change in risk since the area was last audited, the quality of controls, and others.

- External risks may be related to competition, suppliers, or other industry issues.
  - Relevant risk factors may include pending regulatory or legal changes and other political and economic factors.
  - Impacts may be felt through organizational reputation in addition to typical financial impacts.

Once all information is gathered, the CAE develops an internal audit plan, which may include:
- A list of proposed audit engagements and specifications regarding whether the engagements are assurance or consulting in nature.
- The rationale for selecting each proposed engagement.
- Objectives and scope of each proposed engagement.
- A list of initiatives or projects that result from the internal audit strategy but may not be directly related to an internal audit.

Examples of initiatives or projects arising from internal audit strategy but that may not be directly related to internal audit include things like monitoring an ethics hotline or conducting fraud awareness training.

Once the plan is created, the CAE discusses it with the board, senior management, and other stakeholders to create alignment among their priorities. The discussion will also acknowledge material risk areas that are not addressed in the plan.

Sources of Potential Engagements

The Audit Universe

Not all organizations will use the term "audit universe." Generally speaking, however, the audit universe includes:
- Major functions.
- Operations.
- Operating units.
- Subsidiaries.

- Third parties.
- IT.
- Business, service, and product lines.

Each of these is considered an "auditable unit."

The audit universe also includes:
- Any applicable areas (e.g., financial reporting or compliance) that have a pervasive, organization-wide impact and fall under the internal audit "umbrella" from an assurance coverage perspective.
- Relevant regulatory mandates in highly regulated industries.
- Independent compliance assessments of high-risk areas as mandated by government agency examiners, even in the absence of specific laws and regulations requiring them.

There will be a number of functional areas or auditable units that may or may not need auditing in a given audit cycle.

The audit universe is not defined solely by operating entities, their overarching processes, and their related functional activities. It also encompasses the organization's **strategic plan** and the controls management has in place to mitigate risks, achieve organizational goals and objectives, and ensure that stakeholder needs are being met.

The Organization's Strategic Plan

Strategic plans are based on some degree of environmental analysis (environmental scanning) that provides intelligence on what is and what will potentially be happening inside and outside the organization.

Organizations may use a strengths, weaknesses, opportunities, and threats analysis (**SWOT analysis**) to identify and classify elements that can help or hinder the organization or its strategic plans or activities.
- Strength and weakness reviews in SWOT analyses look at the organization's internal capabilities (or lack thereof).
- Opportunities and threats in a SWOT analysis are then focused mostly on external factors that can impact organizational success for good or for ill (perhaps also considering some related internal opportunities or risks).
- Opportunity and threat reviews may look at the following factors:
  - Legal factors
  - Regulatory factors
  - Market forces, industry trends, and the competition
  - Stakeholder groups
  - Technology trends and related internal capabilities
  - Customers

Management and Employees

The risk perspective of executives and key operational managers is important, as they are responsible for:

- Establishing plans.
- Defining risk tolerances.
- Allocating resources to achieve the plans.
- Monitoring the activities being done to achieve the plans.
- Reviewing results.

The employees' perspectives are also important, as employees are closest to the business activities. Both parties can offer valuable insights on the risks the organization faces.

Management may have special projects that should be included in the audit universe. However, the internal audit function must have the competencies and resources required to perform such work for it to be accepted.

Information can be solicited from management and employees in different ways. Three of the most common techniques are:

- Interviews.
- Focus groups.
- Questionnaires/surveys.

Regulatory Mandates

While compliance with some regulations is voluntary, many regulations have the force of law. Some regulatory mandates cut across a variety of industries (such as environmental protection regulations restricting pollution or occupational safety and health regulations protecting workers). Industries may also have unique regulations (such as aviation, banking, or forestry). Privacy regulations, such as the EU's GDPR (General Data Protection Regulation), regulate how companies handle things like customer data. Regulatory factors can also arise from self-regulating bodies and professional societies.

Relevant Market and Industry Trends

Risk issues posed by current industry or economic situations could be valid sources for potential engagements. For example, organizations that are investing heavily in new technologies like artificial intelligence are also creating new risks.

The market for a given product or service has a life cycle, and an industry that produces the product or service will be facing certain trends depending on whether demand needs to be built up, is growing rapidly, is steady, or is in decline. These changes can be driven by:

- Technology changes.
- Customer preference changes.
- Societal shifts.

Internal auditors need to understand the root causes of these changes and what types of pressures these are creating in the areas of risk, governance, and controls, especially in times of rapid growth or times of decline.

Emerging Issues

In the world in which modern organizations operate, there are constantly emerging threats that originate from changes and trends in:

- Technology.
- The environment.
- Society.
- Health and safety (i.e., pandemics).
- Governance.

When identifying sources of potential engagements, the CAE should consider whether emerging issues such in these and other areas are a factor in the organization and its industry.

Other Sources

In some organizations, internal assurance functions (e.g., security, quality, health and safety) or external assurance providers (e.g., external auditors, regulators, partners) may be sources of potential engagements. Internal audit may review areas of weakness identified by these assurance functions and may also evaluate the quality of the assurance functions as part of the audit universe.

Topic B: Leveraging Risk Management Frameworks

This topic discusses how an internal audit activity can determine which risk management framework works best in the context of the current organization and how such frameworks can be used to assign priority levels to potential engagements.

Organizational Risk Management Frameworks

The internal audit activity can work in close cooperation with the risk management function. However, not every organization will have a stand-alone risk management function, so the ability for internal audit to work with risk management will vary from organization to organization.

The first step internal audit should take when identifying a risk management framework is to examine other risk management frameworks in use throughout the organization, to avoid the need to create or deploy one from scratch.

If there aren't other viable frameworks in use, the organization can choose from several options, including:
* Using third-party frameworks such as COSO ERM.
* Developing their own framework in-house.

It is important to remember that the internal audit activity cannot give objective assurance on any part of a risk management framework it has designed.

Prioritizing Audit Engagements

Most internal audit functions perform annual and engagement risk-based assessment activities to help prioritize risks according to their potential impacts on the organization's achievement of goals and objectives.
* At the macro level, these activities help with developing a proposed audit plan to submit to the board.
* At the micro level, these activities help prioritize the scope of audit work and assurance being provided by internal audit engagements.

The risk assessment activities may be used to prioritize audit engagements through the use of an assurance map.

An assurance map is a matrix comprising a visual representation of the organization's risks and all the internal and external providers of assurance services that cover those risks. It may be used to coordinate the timing and scope of activities or as a basis for discussing whether reliance on the work of other assurance providers would be appropriate. Senior management may also use the map to ensure that risk management and internal control functions are properly aligned and effectively monitored.

Assurance mapping steps include:
1. Identifying sources of risk information.
2. Organizing risks into categories for consolidated viewing.
3. Identifying assurance providers.

4. Gathering information and documenting assurance activities by risk categories.
5. Periodically reviewing, monitoring, and updating the assurance map.

Exhibit 2-1 shows a pared-down example of an assurance map. An actual assurance map may feature more rows and columns and additional risk category groupings.

Exhibit 2-1: Assurance Map

Risk categories	Management 1st Line			Functional oversight 2nd Line			Independent 3rd Line	
	Finance	Human resources	Treasury	Risk managemenet processes	Perfomance review commitee	Safety review board	Internal audit	Outside quality auditors
Regulatory compliance & reporting								
Disclosure	Total	Total	Total	Partial			Limited	
Environmental				Partial			Total	
Information privacy							Total	
Technology								
Data security							Partial	
Hardware availability & effectiveness				Limited				
Software usability & efficiency								

Total risk coverage

Limited or no risk coverage

Partial risk coverage

Risk area outside function's mandate

Topic C: Assurance Engagements

This topic takes a deep look into the various types of assurance engagements, including the objectives, stakeholders, and risks associated with each type.

Types of Assurance Engagements

Assurance services are an objective examination of the evidence for the purpose of providing an independent assessment on governance, risk management, and control processes of the organization. This topic discusses the following types of assurance engagements:

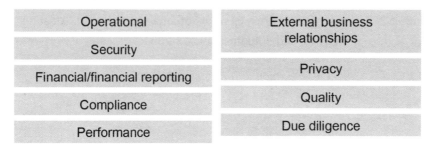

Operational	External business relationships
Security	
Financial/financial reporting	Privacy
Compliance	Quality
Performance	Due diligence

For each type of audit, the following aspects are discussed:
• Objectives
• Stakeholders
• Risks

Operational Engagements

Operational audits are focused on providing assurance on governance, risk management, and controls in regard to the effectiveness and efficiency of operations. They are not focused on finance or compliance in particular, although those types of risks may be included, and they may examine anything about the organization with an underlying business process. Such engagements may be referred to as management audits in government environments.

Objectives

Specific objectives will depend on the organization, process, or activity under audit. Three key considerations in reaching an evaluation of the overall effectiveness of the governance, risk management, and control processes associated with a given business process are:
• Were significant discrepancies or weaknesses discovered from the audit work performed and other assessment information gathered?
• If so, were corrections or improvements made after the discoveries?
• Do the discoveries and their consequences lead to the conclusion that a pervasive condition exists resulting in an unacceptable level of business risk?

Stakeholders

Stakeholders include:
• The board and management who are ultimately responsible for oversight.
• Specific business process owners who will be responsible for addressing audit recommendations.

Risks

Risks related to operational effectiveness include business processes that fail to work toward or are counterproductive to organizational objectives. Risks related to inefficiency involve achieving goals in a manner that is more costly than the value that is added or a selected benchmark.

Suboptimization can affect both efficiency and effectiveness. It involves focusing on optimizing a particular business process or unit at the expense of the overall organizational goals, often caused by a departmental "silo" mentality.

Security Engagements

The security aspects of a business are critical and an important part of internal auditing.

Objectives

Security audits primarily focus on governance, risks, and controls related to:
- Safeguarding of assets.
- Reliability and integrity of information.

Stakeholders

Security audits can span the operations and facilities or can be focused on one subject, such as information technology security or head office security. Therefore, stakeholders will include all parties directly responsible for the security of the area to be audited, including security guards, if any, and IT professionals.

The board and management have ultimate responsibility and are the stakeholders to whom the CAE reports all security issues and recommendations.

Risks

A security policy might include control systems and standards to manage security within acceptable limits in regard to the following risks:
- Unauthorized physical access to or attack on a facility or organizational personnel
- Theft of or willful damage to products, inventory, supplies, assets, or information
- Fraud by employees or third parties

These concerns can be influenced by other industry- or region-specific risks:
- Inherent industry risks
- Inherent social and political risks

- Market and economy pressures
- Location and facility risks
- Natural hazards (such as fires, floods, earthquakes, or animals) and biohazards

The policy could include standards and guidance in regard to risks and issues such as:
- Terrorism, including active shooters, bomb threats, and so on.
- Addictions (e.g., drugs, alcohol, gambling).
- Weapons.
- Travel.
- Executive protection, including kidnapping or extortion.
- Crisis management.
- Cameras and electronic monitoring.
- Intrusion detection.
- Facility design and construction.
- Investigations or searches.
- Use of third-party security services.
- Other issues specific to the risks of the organization.

Financial and Financial Reporting Engagements

Internal and external audit coordination and reliance efforts can play a major role in providing the most effective and efficient overall assurance coverage for public-company internal controls over financial reporting (ICFR) audits.

- Financial audits performed by external auditors focus on the fairness of an organization's financial statements and ICFR, if applicable (i.e., for audits of public companies).

- Financial audits performed by internal auditors primarily focus on assurance over internal controls but may also review the quality and usefulness of the organization's managerial accounting and internal reporting systems. Assurance on internal controls may be needed because of rules over the quality of those controls.

Objectives

External financial reporting is historical in nature, so its objective is to prepare relevant and reliable financial statements that fairly and accurately represent the recent historical activities of the organization.

Financial reporting objectives should form the basis for the majority of internal controls. Internal controls set reliable financial reporting as a key objective because of the importance of these reports to lenders (primarily bankers) and investors and because of their role in satisfying legal and regulatory requirements and in ensuring efficiency and stewardship over the organization's resources.

The objective of assurance audits of ICFR is to provide assurance regarding the effectiveness of the processes and procedures (controls) that help the organization's financial reporting to be:

- Reliable.
- Timely.
- Transparent.
- Complete.

Assurance audits of managerial accounting and reporting systems feature similar objectives as those stated above for audits of ICFR, but they are intended to be shared with management to enable effective decision making within the organization.

Regulations around the world have increased focus on internal auditor responsibilities in the area of financial audits.

Stakeholders

Main stakeholders include:

- The board.
- The audit committee.
- Senior management (especially the CEO and the CFO).

Senior management is the owner of the control environment and financial information, including the footnotes and disclosures, which are integral to the financial statements.

Other stakeholders include:

- Regulators.
- Rating agencies.
- Current and potential stockholders.
- Investors.
- Bankers.
- External auditors.
- Interested parties.

Risks

The internal audit activity's work plans and specific assurance engagements begin with a careful identification of the exposures facing the organization. The work plan is based on the risks and the assessment of the risk management and control processes maintained by management to mitigate those risks.

Among the events and transactions included in the identification of risks are:

- New businesses—including mergers and acquisitions.
- New products and systems.
- Joint ventures and partnerships.
- Restructuring.
- Management estimates, budgets, and forecasts.
- Regulatory compliance.
- Fraud risks—often from overstating revenues or assets and/or understating expenses or liabilities.

Compliance Engagements

Compliance is "the conformity and adherence to policies, plans, procedures, laws, regulations, contracts, or other requirements." Compliance audits evaluate the adequacy and effectiveness of controls that keep the organization in compliance with applicable laws and regulations, contracts, and the organization's own policies.

Objectives

The objectives of an effective compliance program are to:

- Identify and discourage intentional and unintentional violations.
- Detect illegal activities.
- Ensure that adequate organization-wide compliance training programs are in place.
- Assist in proving insurance claims.
- Encourage proper behavior by providing incentives.
- Enhance and create corporate identity.

The organization should establish compliance standards and procedures that are reasonably capable of reducing the prospect of criminal conduct by employees and other agents, and compliance audits should review and assess these standards/procedures.

Internal audit scope may include a review of the compliance programs to see if:

- Written materials are effective.
- Employees have received communications.
- Detected violations have been handled appropriately.
- Discipline has been even-handed.
- Whistleblowers have not suffered retaliation.
- The overall compliance function has fulfilled its responsibilities.

Stakeholders

Stakeholders include:
- The board.
- Management (may include a chief compliance officer in large organizations).
- Compliance professionals.
- Process owners and workers who are responsible for day-to-day compliance.

Risks

While there are many types of regulations and policies, each with its own risks, environmental compliance risks can be used as a representative example. Environmental health and safety (EH&S) risks to consider in audit planning include ineffective organizational reporting structures; the likelihood of causing environmental harm; damage to the health and safety of workers, customers, or the community; fines and penalties; expenditures mandated by environmental or health and safety agencies; and negative publicity and loss of reputation and public image.

Performance Engagements

Performance audit engagements assess whether management has appropriate, necessary, and sufficient monitoring and controlling activities in place to assess how the following areas are performing in pursuit of meeting strategic, tactical, and/or operational objectives and goals:
- The organization as a whole
- Specific units or functional areas
- Specific job roles or individuals

The audits can also determine whether the information is:
- Gathered and analyzed in a timely enough fashion to be useful.
- Being leveraged for informed decision making and management control.

Performance reporting functions can also be audited.

It is important to realize that not all aspects of an organization can be efficiently and effectively tracked. Standards and key performance indicators should be designed and written in a way that will allow personnel to measure progress toward meeting the organization's most important objectives.

Objectives

The objectives of performance monitoring, reporting, and controlling are to:
- Accurately measure performance in areas that relate to key business objectives.
- Gather and prepare sufficient and useful information efficiently and in a timely fashion.
- Use the information effectively for management control.

Performance audit engagements might determine whether:
- The right things are being measured.
- The measurement process is efficient and is being performed correctly.
- Data is collected and analyzed per the desired schedule.
- Reports highlight the critical information needed for control.
- The information is being used to make informed decisions.

Stakeholders

Stakeholders for performance audits include the board and management who require accurate and timely performance information to make corrections as well as any internal or external party or entity that is being measured. Stakeholders who are being measured for performance want to be judged against criteria that they can personally control to some degree. They also want to know how they are being measured so they can have a reasonable chance of success and improvement.

Risks

What can be measured can be managed, so failure to measure performance introduces the risk that performance cannot be managed. Other risks include:
- Measuring the wrong key performance indicators so that workers or processes fail to work toward organizational goals or objectives.
- Receiving information too late to be of use.
- Measuring too many performance indicators rather than just the key ones.

Persons and processes that are not managed can quickly get out of control, and the results can include missed budgets or deadlines, accidents, lawsuits, increased insurance premiums, and loss of worker productivity.

External Business Relationship Audits

"External business partners," "extended relationships," and "contractual relationships" are among the numerous names by which today's organizations define their **external business relationships (EBRs)**.

Examples of EBRs include:
- Joint venture partners.
- Outsourced service providers.
- Agents.
- Contract workers.
- Vendors.
- Franchisees.

When contemplating the internal audit activity's EBR responsibilities, consider the following:

- Organizations have multiple EBRs that satisfy a number of business requirements.
- Each relationship generates risks.
- It is management's responsibility to manage these risks and achieve the benefits of the relationship.
- Internal auditing plays an important role in helping management and validating their efforts.

Internal audits of EBRs range from an audit of a single contract or relationship to an audit of an overall process that includes some organizational processes and some EBR processes. Audits of EBRs often take the form of contract assurance. A **contract** is an agreement between parties, with terms and conditions that describe the agreement and constitute a legal obligation.

Objectives

Internal auditors need to understand all the elements associated with EBRs, including:

- Initiating a relationship.
- Contracting and defining a relationship.
- Procurement.
- Managing and monitoring the continued relationship (including control environment considerations of the objectivity and independence of those responsible for managing and monitoring).
- Discontinuing the relationship.

After understanding the expectations of both parties, along with the appropriate processes to manage and monitor the relationship, the internal auditor develops an appropriate internal audit program with relevant audit objectives for internal audits of external relationships. In addition, internal audit procedures may include elements of evaluating adherence to (and compliance with) contractual terms to determine whether monetary and nonmonetary obligations are met.

Third and independent parties may audit the organization for the same purposes.

Stakeholders

Stakeholders for audits of third parties include the organization and the third party as well as individuals responsible for approving and signing contracts. Those responsible for managing the EBRs and monitoring and enforcing contract compliance need to be specified in each organization. Other stakeholders include:

- Internal auditors.
- Legal counsel.
- Individuals responsible for providing inputs to or receiving outputs from the third party under contract.

Courts of law may be considered another stakeholder, since this is the ultimate forum for interpreting contract language and compliance.

Risks

Risks for external business relationships include all of the risks of the business process that is being outsourced, since the end result is still the organization's responsibility. The organization will be held responsible for the actions of its partners and perhaps even for the partners of those partners (i.e., the third tier in the supply chain). Contracts can help transfer some of this risk, but other risks, such as reputation risk, cannot be transferred.

Organizations monitor and manage EBR risks, and failure to do so properly is another risk. Other risks revolve around:

- The process of finding the most appropriate partners.
- Establishing controls over partners and contract management.
- Contract compliance auditing.
- Customer and supplier relationship management.

These are the risks of having ineffective, inefficient, or negative business relationships. Internal auditors can perform due diligence audits at the start of a relationship to determine the risks of the EBR misrepresenting the organization's values.

Another risk is that not all EBRs are formally arranged and documented. For example, a procurement professional could have a relationship with an unofficial supplier that weakens the official purchasing contract relationships. Poor partner accounting or reporting is also a risk; this could impact the organization's required accounting (e.g., there could be uncollected revenues) and reporting (e.g., the organization could be unable to verify if a certain toxic substance is found in supplier subcomponents).

Internal auditors also have a role to play in verifying that the EBR has sufficient and effective insurance to address insurable risks. This may include:

- Workers' compensation coverage.
- Coverage for liability to the public or of professionals.
- Vehicle insurance.

EBRs may have conflicts of interest such as also working with a competitor. Requiring conflict-of-interest disclosures may allow some relationships to continue if they are within the organization's risk tolerance level.

Intellectual property (IP) may also be at risk in any EBR relationship in which the organization must share confidential information. Clear contracts can reduce the risks of theft of IP or the associated revenue streams, but the contracts may not be enforceable in some countries. Contracts can be designed to share the risk of poor IP control with the EBR, such as a mutual loss of revenue.

Privacy Engagements

Privacy can be simply defined as the protection of the collection, storage, processing, dissemination, and destruction of personal information, but it can mean many things to many people. Privacy definitions in the business environment vary widely depending upon:
- Country.
- Culture.
- Political environment.
- Legal framework.

The many definitions of privacy can be used by any organization to guide its privacy program.

Personal information generally refers to information that is associated with a specific individual or that has identifying characteristics that, when combined with other information, can be associated with a specific individual. It can include any factual or subjective information—recorded or not—in any medium. Personal information could include:
- Names, addresses, identification numbers, family relationships.
- Employee files, evaluations, comments, social status, or disciplinary actions.
- Credit records, income, financial status.
- Medical status.

Objectives

In addition to the typical steps required for an audit, there are additional aspects the CAE should take into account with privacy audits, including:
- Possible privacy breaches.
- Staff management and record retention issues.
- Privacy assessments performed by other assurance providers.

Many of these aspects are covered by practices of the internal and external audit professions.

An organization's governing body is responsible for deciding the risk it is willing to take and for ensuring that resources are in place to manage risk according to that appetite. Addressing privacy risks includes establishing an appropriate privacy framework consisting of policies, procedures, and controls. Internal audit can evaluate that framework, identify significant risks, and make appropriate recommendations to enhance the privacy framework.

Stakeholders

Stakeholders for privacy issues start with the board and its audit committee. These parties are responsible for oversight of all aspects of privacy relevant to the organization. Next, senior and operating management are ultimately accountable for assessing risks and implementing privacy controls. Other stakeholders include anyone who could be affected by a breach in privacy controls, including:
- Customers.
- Employees.
- The organization.
- Business partners.

Other oversight groups may exist.

Risks

Protection of privacy is a very serious risk management issue for organizations. The failure to protect personal information with appropriate controls can have significant consequences, including:
- Damage to the reputation of individuals and/or the organization.
- Organizational exposure to legal liability.
- Sanctions imposed by regulators.
- Allegations of deceptive practices.
- Diminished customer and/or employee trust.

Risks associated with the privacy of information encompass:
- Personal privacy (physical and psychological).
- Privacy of space (freedom from surveillance).
- Privacy of communication (freedom from monitoring).
- Privacy of information (collection, use, and disclosure of personal information by others).

Privacy risks may also include impairment of the organization's brand and public image, followed by potential losses of market share and customers, leading to potential losses for investors or the organization.

Quality Engagements

Achieving and continually improving quality is a significant endeavor for an organization. Auditors measure an organization's current operations against a set of standards or other criteria. Essentially, they assess the quality of the organization's controls and determine if controls are being updated and enhanced as organizational activities and industry practices change and as technology is enhanced over time.

Objectives

The objective of a quality audit engagement is to help an organization improve its quality and productivity by providing assurance that the organization's quality and continuous improvement plans are such that, if followed, the desired quality will be attained.

Quality needs to start at the beginning of a process and needs to be considered throughout, until completion. This may take the form of conformance to a methodology such as total quality management (TQM).

A related objective is to provide assurance that the internal audit function is functioning at the desired quality level for the board and management, as was discussed in Part 1, Section IV, on quality assurance and improvement programs.

A quality audit provides management with the necessary information to:
- Recognize actual or potential risks.
- Make appropriate decisions so the costs of quality (discussed below) can be prevented or rectified.
- Identify areas of opportunity for continuous improvement.
- Assess the quality of staff training.
- Verify compliance with the organization's processes and procedures as well as any regulatory or legal requirements.
- Justify the expenditures on quality activities by assessing the actual savings achieved.
- Eliminate outdated activities and unnecessary controls.

The organization uses this information for continuous improvement of its controls and standards.

Stakeholders

All members of the organization must be involved for the organization to achieve:
- Long-term success.
- Customer satisfaction.
- Positive benefits for its members and society at large.

Specific persons should be responsible and accountable for specific quality aspects. Management and the board are ultimately responsible for control and oversight.

Risks

The risks of poor quality are often called the costs of quality. The costs of quality are the activities associated with poor quality:

- Prevention
- Identification
- Repair
- Rectification

They also include the opportunity costs from lost production time and lost sales as a result of poor quality. Exhibit 2-2 lists some of the most common costs of quality.

Exhibit 2-2: Costs of Quality

Quality Cost Type	Quality Cost Components
Prevention costs (incurred to eliminate defective products before they are produced)	• Reengineering and design • Use of high-quality parts • Improved processes • Employee training
Appraisal costs (incurred to evaluate purchased materials, processes, products, and services to ensure conformance to specifications)	• Assessment and approval of suppliers of products and services • Inspecting and testing raw materials received from suppliers and work-in-process (WIP) inventory • Inspecting WIP at vulnerable, high-risk points in the production process
Internal failure costs (incurred when defects are discovered before sending products to customers)	• Handling and fixing products or disposing of them • Opportunity cost of not being able to sell disposed-of products
External failure costs (incurred when customer receives defective products)	• Cost of returns • Warranty work • Product liability claims • Opportunity cost of lost sales from damaged reputation

Due Diligence Audits

Due diligence is the process of investigating a person, business, or financial transaction to establish the value of the entity or transaction and the cost of any associated liabilities. The investigation should identify the presence of certain risks or confirm the absence of such risks. A due diligence audit may refer to either an investigation of an entity/transaction or an audit of the due diligence investigation process itself.

The most common situations for performing due diligence audits are those involving:
- Financial activities (banking, securities, mergers or acquisitions).
- Real estate (property, structures).
- Intellectual property.

Objectives

Due diligence investigations are often undertaken by persons or organizations when they are interested in acquiring another business or property or are otherwise becoming involved in a financial transaction. The results of the investigation are used to decide whether or not to:
- Purchase real estate.
- Enter into a lease.
- Enter into a business partnership, joint venture, merger, consolidation, or other similar arrangement.

Therefore, common objectives of a due diligence audit are to ensure that a proposed action such as a merger will:
- Enhance the value of the organization.
- Be consistent with strategic objectives.
- Avoid hidden liabilities.

Stakeholders

Stakeholders to a due diligence audit include the person or entity being reviewed, because the process could reveal potentially damaging information that should be handled confidentially so as not to cause harm to that person's or entity's reputation. Other key stakeholders include:
- The management decision maker involved in the potential new relationship or merger/acquisition.
- The board.
- The legal department.
- Related business process owners.
- Any consultants or advisors.

Risks

Whenever due diligence is discussed, due care is also mentioned. **Due care** is the level of caution exercised when performing the due diligence audit and reporting the results. Basically, did the internal auditor do what any reasonable person would do?

Other risks related to poor due diligence include harm to the organization's reputation if it is associated with an individual or entity that is later found to have engaged in illegal or unethical activities that should have been discovered earlier. The acquiring organization's revenue and profits may be harmed if the acquired organization has inflated its revenues and profits.

Topic D: Consulting Engagements

This topic covers the various types of consulting engagements and the purpose they play in the internal audit activity and the organization at large.

Purpose of Consulting Engagements

Recall that consulting services are advisory in nature and are generally performed at the specific request of an engagement client. Consulting services generally involve two parties:
- The person or group offering the advice
- The person or group seeking and receiving the advice

When performing consulting services, the internal auditor should maintain objectivity and not assume management responsibility.

As indicated in Implementation Standard 1000.C1, the nature of the consulting services that an internal audit activity undertakes must be defined in the audit charter. This ensures that the board and senior management are made aware of and authorize the kinds of work that internal auditors are performing.

Implementation Standard 1000.C1 (Consulting Engagements)
The nature of consulting services must be defined in the internal audit charter.

Consulting and related client services activities are intended to add value and improve an organization's governance, risk management, and control processes without the internal auditor assuming management responsibility.

The quantity and kind vary widely. The CAE is responsible for allocating audit resources to projects that create the highest value for the organization. When determining whether or not to provide consulting services, the first consulting role internal audit should play is determining if the first or second lines of defense are responsible or better equipped to provide the service.

There are three main types of consulting engagements: advisory, training, and facilitative.

Advisory Consulting Engagements

Advisory consulting engagements offer advice. Examples of advisory engagements include:

- Advising on control design.
- Advising during development of policies and procedures.
- Participating in an advisory role for high-risk projects.
- Advising on security breaches or business continuity interruptions.
- Advising on certain enterprise risk management activities.

Let's look in depth at a few examples of advisory consulting engagements—systems development life cycle review, due diligence, and privacy.

Systems Development Life Cycle Review

Systems development life cycle (SDLC) reviews may be either advisory or facilitative in nature, but they are most often conducted as advisory engagements.

The SDLC review should involve all stakeholders in the system—all those who have an organizational interest in the day-to-day operations of the system. The auditor has significant responsibilities during the SDLC review:

- Ensuring that stakeholder interests are at the forefront of the development objectives
- Ensuring that the development project follows the organization's standards for systems development
- Ensuring that the IT activity adheres to a framework or methodology such as the SDLC

Exhibit 2-3 shows a typical systems development life cycle. (Other models exist.)

Exhibit 2-3: Systems Development Life Cycle

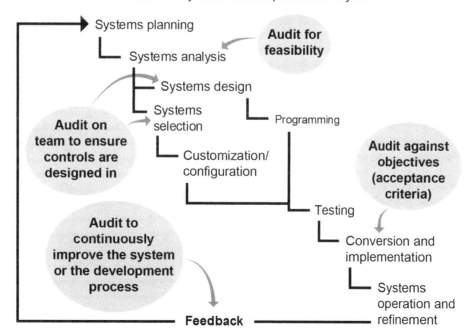

v7.0

Auditors could be involved in a design review at several places:
- During systems analysis as a project team member to define the goals or purposes of a procedure or business function and to identify ways to accomplish those goals most efficiently, to evaluate the feasibility of proposed systems (to determine if a project will add value and satisfy objectives at a reasonable cost), or to evaluate the feasibility assessment process itself
- During system design or system selection as a project team member to ensure that controls are designed in
- During conversion and implementation to ensure that the project meets objectives and acceptance criteria
- During feedback as part of a post-project design or acquisition review for continuous improvement of the system and/or the process in general

Systems analysis is a key phase of the SDLC, and this is often where internal auditors play a key role in a consulting engagement. Systems analysis may involve applying problem-solving methodologies and a system-wide perspective and/or deconstructing the parts and subparts of the system to gain an understanding of how the system or process works in detail.

Systems design is the process of defining the architecture, modules, interfaces, and data for a system to satisfy the organization's requirements for the system. Internal auditors may be able to take their holistic view of organizational processes and the overall goals of the process identified in systems analysis to help ensure that systems design is comprehensive and that the overall architecture or framework is sound. Systems design can be seen as an extension of systems theory (understanding the system as a whole, the cyclic nature of many processes, and the role of its inputs and outputs) into the realm of product development.

Due Diligence

Since due diligence was addressed in the prior topic, it is not covered in detail here. In a consultative capacity, internal audit may provide advice and insight regarding a proposed transaction's contributions to the organization's strategic objectives and the transaction's impact on ongoing core business activities.

Privacy

Like due diligence, privacy was addressed in detail in the previous topic. A privacy consulting engagement will have considerable overlap with a privacy assurance engagement. Internal audit can:
- Help keep the organization up-to-date on the latest trends, regulations, and controls.
- Leverage its holistic perspective of the organization to provide valuable advice to management and the board regarding the most appropriate privacy framework and the most cost-effective investments in privacy.

Training Consulting Engagements

Training consulting engagements occur when internal audit personnel are asked to serve as educators for certain areas of the organization, based on their specialized knowledge. Examples of training engagements include:

- Training on risk management and internal control.
- Post-mortem analysis.
- Business process mapping.

Let's take a closer look at business process mapping and internal control training.

Business Process Mapping

Business process mapping is often used in consulting engagements as a method of understanding what is really needed to make a business process function versus what is being done but isn't adding any value to the end customer. Business process mapping often begins with a process owner leading the internal auditor on a walkthrough. Then a flowcharting activity is conducted to map the process and identify where value is added and where business process improvements could be made. Additional details on process mapping, including performing walkthroughs and flowcharting, are covered elsewhere in this product.

Internal Control Training

Providing audit clients with the opportunity to attend a well-structured workshop on internal controls or the COSO internal control framework may:

- Help them understand the importance of audits of internal controls.
- Make them more comfortable with the process and more willing to provide useful, complete information.

Knowledge of the components of internal controls and the related principles help clients to understand the necessary management activities to be evaluated in making a conclusion on the quality of internal controls.

Delivering this type of training helps:

- Audit clients better understand the importance of internal control related to their job responsibilities, helping the organization achieve its objectives.
- Internal audit activities to be understood and better received by the clients being audited.

Facilitative Consulting Engagements

Facilitative consulting engagements require the internal audit function to be more involved with the activity in question rather that just offering the necessary knowledge for an individual outside of the function to carry out a task. Examples of facilitative engagements include:

- Facilitating the organization's risk assessment process.
- Benchmarking internal areas with comparable areas of other similar organizations.
- Facilitating management's control self-assessment.
- Facilitating a task force charged with redesigning controls or procedures.
- Acting as a liaison between management and the independent outside auditors, government agencies, vendors, and contractors.
- Facilitating discussion on a post-mortem of a major systems or process interruption.

Let's examine benchmarking and control self-assessments more closely.

Benchmarking

A benchmark is simply a goal that an organization (or person) aims to achieve. In **benchmarking**, a benchmark is measured against an internal or external group for the purpose of determining areas for potential improvement and to identify best practices. Internal benchmarks include:

- Historical data.
- Goals and objectives.

External benchmarks include:

- Industry standards.
- Best practices.
- Regulatory requirements.

Evaluating the benchmarks set by clients within the organization is a service appropriate for internal auditors to provide. Benchmarking is especially appropriate in performance and quality audits. (Benchmarking is in fact associated with total quality management.)

Classifications of Benchmarking

There are several widely accepted ways of selecting benchmarks that are measurable, precise, meaningful, and realistic. Common classifications for benchmarking activities include the following:

- **Internal benchmarking**. Comparing similar information within a process or entity, either achievable performance above a current baseline or stellar practice.
- **Competitive benchmarking**. Comparing measures with similar measures of direct competitors, locally, nationally, or worldwide.
- **Industry benchmarking**. Comparing processes to similar processes in the same industry.
- **Functional benchmarking**. Comparing related functions in the same technical area to show what is being achieved in other industries.

- **Generic benchmarking**. Comparing processes in one operation against processes with similar features but in another industry.
- **Best-in-class benchmarking**. Comparing measures with those of organizations that are best in class for a function.

Control Self-Assessment (CSA)

While the term "assessment" is generally associated with assurance more than consulting, internal auditors may play a role in control self-assessments (a type of consulting activity), primarily in the role of facilitators. Internal auditors may also be called on to provide subject matter knowledge in the areas of internal controls and control-related considerations.

A CSA is a process whereby employee teams and management, at local and executive levels, continuously maintain awareness of all material factors affecting the likelihood of achieving the organization's objectives, thereby enabling them to make appropriate adjustments. To promote independence, objectivity, and quality within the process, as well as effective governance, it is desirable that internal auditors be involved in the process and that they independently report results to senior management and board committees.

A CSA is a useful and efficient approach for managers and internal auditors to use in collaborating to assess and evaluate control procedures. In its purest form, a CSA integrates business objectives and risks with control processes.

Blended Engagements

Blended engagements incorporate elements of both consulting and assurance services. Care must be taken that neither independence nor objectivity is compromised. It is often necessary to communicate outcomes of these engagements separately.

Topic E: Other Party Coordination

This topic covers the process that the internal audit activity employs when partnering with internal and external providers and how to determine what level of reliance to place on the work of the partners.

In addition to reviewing the contents of this topic, students can review the following IIA materials:
- Implementation Guidance for Standard 2050
- Practice Guide, "Coordination and Reliance: Developing an Assurance Map"
- Practice Guide, "Reliance by Internal Audit on Other Assurance Providers"
- Practice Guide, "Coordinating Risk Management and Assurance"

Coordination and Reliance

 Performance Standard 2050, "Coordination and Reliance"

The chief audit executive should share information, coordinate activities, and consider relying upon the work of other internal and external assurance and consulting service providers to ensure proper coverage and minimize duplication of efforts.

Standard 2050 requires the CAE's inclusion and participation in the organization's assurance provider framework. A consistent process for the basis of reliance on other assurance and consulting providers should be established. This process should consider the following with regard to assurance providers:

- Purpose
- Objectivity
- Competence
- Elements of practice
- Impact

As the assurance provider puts each of these principles into practice, the CAE can place higher reliance on the provider's work.

The CAE should have a clear understanding of the work performed by other providers of assurance and consulting services, including the:

- Scope.
- Objectives.
- Results.

Where reliance is placed on the work of others, the CAE is still accountable and responsible for ensuring adequate support for conclusions and opinions reached.

Internal providers include oversight functions that either report to senior management or are part of senior management. They are often considered the "second line of defense." These providers may be involved in:

- Environmental issues.
- Financial control.
- Health and safety.
- IT security.
- Legal issues.
- Risk management.
- Compliance.
- Quality assurance.

External providers may report to senior management or external stakeholders, or they could be hired by and report to the CAE.

An assurance map can be used by the CAE during this process to support collaboration among assurance providers and to facilitate the efficient and effective use of resources. It can serve as the first step in developing a plan for reliance.

Once providers of assurance and consulting services have been identified, the CAE considers the type and amount of information that may be shared with them, in accordance with confidentiality requirements. Coordination processes vary by organization. They may be informal in small organizations or formal and complex in larger ones.

Formal coordination processes include:
- Regular sharing of reports and the outcomes of assurance activities.
- Discussion and review of techniques and methods used to reach conclusions.

The CAE may develop an annual report discussing:
- The assurance framework.
- How the assurance framework is being employed.
- The results of assurance engagements to be shared with the organization's board and executive management team. Results may also be distributed through the organization's governance or risk management function.

The CAE must have a consistent process and a set of criteria to determine whether the internal audit activity may rely on the work of another provider. This process may include:
- Evaluating objectivity.
- Considering independence.
- Confirming competency.
- Assessing due professional care.
- Gaining an understanding of the scope, objectives, and results of the actual work performed.

Conformance with Standard 2050 may be demonstrated in communications regarding distinct assurance and consulting roles and responsibilities. Conformance regarding the reliance on the work of other providers may be evidenced through the CAE's documentation of the process and criteria applied.

Coordinating with External Assurance

Examples of common external assurance providers include:
- Public accounting firms.
- Government auditor general offices.
- Consulting companies.
- Legal firms.

- Security organizations.
- Internal audit activities of service providers.
- Internal audit activities of user entities.

It is important for management and the CAE to understand the relevance of assurance work completed by external assurance providers within the organization.

Common questions that should be asked when coordinating with assurance functions from outside organizations include the following:

- Are the external assurance providers sufficiently qualified, objective, and independent to perform the necessary assurance work?
- What is the impact to the annual internal audit plan if the CAE either places reliance or does not place reliance on the work of external assurance providers?
- Do the objectives and scope of work performed by external assurance providers address key risks of the organization?
- Should internal audit complete additional assurance work to supplement the work of external assurance providers?
- Should internal audit reperform audit work completed by external assurance providers?
- Should the CAE pursue cosourcing arrangements with external assurance providers?

Chapter 3: Communicating and Reporting

The CAE is responsible for communicating with senior management and the board, as discussed in this chapter. The CAE's completion of these professional responsibilities is made evident by periodically reporting the results of ongoing internal audit activities to senior management and the audit committee during routinely scheduled meetings throughout the year.

Topic A: CAE Annual Audit Plan Communication

This topic discusses the CAE's duty to discuss the annual audit plan with senior management and the board and how significant changes to the plan should be handled.

In addition to reviewing the contents of this topic, students can review the following IIA materials:
- Implementation Guidance for Standard 2020

Communicating the Annual Audit Plan

Performance Standard 2020, "Communication and Approval"

The chief audit executive must communicate the internal audit activity's plans and resource requirements, including significant interim changes, to senior management and the board for review and approval. The chief audit executive must also communicate the impact of resource limitations.

Prior to communicating the audit plan, the CAE must determine the resources needed to implement the plan, based on the risk-based priorities identified during the planning process.

Resources include:
- People.
- Technology.
- Funding.

Note that in accordance with Standard 2010.C1, any accepted consulting engagements must be included in the plan. The resources planned for these consulting engagements should be accounted for in the resource plan.

A portion of the available resources is typically saved to address unplanned changes to the audit plan. Unplanned changes may come from:
- Unanticipated risks.
- Requests for consulting engagements from senior management and/or the board.

It is helpful for the CAE, the board, and senior management to agree in advance on the criteria that would characterize a significant enough change to warrant changes to the audit plan and how those are communicated.

Resource estimates are typically based on experience or comparisons to a similar project. Once created, they can then be compared with available resources to identify potential gaps.

Before formally presenting the annual audit plan to the board for approval, the CAE typically meets with individual senior executives to solicit their input. The CAE can:
- Address any concerns the executives express.
- Incorporate their feedback as needed.
- Obtain their support.
- Gather more information about the timing of proposed engagements and the availability of resources.

Gaining Board Approval

The CAE's presentation to the board may include:

- A list of proposed audit engagements.
- A rationale for selecting each proposed engagement.
- The objectives and scope of each proposed engagement.
- A list of initiatives or projects that result from the internal audit strategy but may not be linked directly to an engagement.
- Discussion of the proposed internal audit plan and the risk assessment on which it is based. This discussion will indicate the risks that will be addressed as well as those that cannot be addressed due to resource constraints.

Ultimately, the engagement plan should address and support the most effective use of internal audit resources. The board or audit committee may make suggestions for changes. Once approved, the CAE should communicate the plan and resource requirements to senior management to give them sufficient time to include the plan requirements in the overall budget and so on.

Conformance with Standard 2020

Conformance with Standard 2020 can be demonstrated by keeping records of the distribution of the internal audit plan, a copy of the board meeting materials that includes the internal audit plan as presented, memos, emails, or notes that document internal discussions.

Topic B: Significant GRC Issue Reporting

This topic discusses the reporting responsibilities that the CAE has regarding significant risk, control, and governance issues that are uncovered by internal audit, including what should be reported, to whom, and how often the reports should take place.

In addition to reviewing the contents of this topic, students can review the following IIA materials:
- Implementation Guidance for Standard 2060

Reporting Significant GRC Issues

Performance Standard 2060, "Reporting to Senior Management and the Board"

The chief audit executive must report periodically to senior management and the board on the internal audit activity's purpose, authority, responsibility, and performance relative to its plan and on its conformance with the Code of Ethics and the *Standards*. Reporting must also include significant risk and control issues, including fraud risks, governance issues, and other matters that require the attention of senior management and/or the board.

It is the CAE's responsibility to periodically review the tenets of the internal audit charter and determine whether the stated purpose, authority, and responsibility continue to enable the internal audit activity to accomplish its objectives. The CAE should communicate the results of this periodic assessment to senior management and the board.

The frequency and content of the reporting are determined collaboratively by the CAE, senior management, and the board. This decision depends on the:

- Importance of the information.
- Urgency of the related actions to be taken.

In implementing the *Standards* related to communication, the CAE will usually want to understand the reporting-related expectations for senior management and the board, which may be stated in the audit committee charter.

In addition to determining the frequency and content of reporting, the three parties typically discuss the importance and urgency of various types of audit information. They may also agree in advance on:

- Protocols for the CAE to report important and urgent risk or control events.
- Related actions to be taken by senior management and the board.

Significant Risk and Control Issues and Management's Acceptance of Risk

Standard 2060 identifies the CAE's responsibility to report significant risk and control issues that could adversely affect the organization. Significant issues may include:

- Conflicts of interest.
- Control weaknesses.
- Errors.
- Fraud.
- Illegal acts.
- Ineffectiveness.
- Inefficiency.

v7.0

If the CAE believes that senior management has accepted a level of risk that the organization would consider unacceptable, the CAE should first attempt to resolve the matter with senior management. If that fails, the CAE should communicate the matter to the board.

Topic C: Risk and Control Process Effectiveness Reporting

This topic discusses what the CAE must report to senior management and the board and how the CAE can use his or her position to help educate senior management and board members unfamiliar with concepts related to risk management.

 In addition to reviewing the contents of this topic, students can review the following IIA materials:
- Implementation Guidance for Standard 2060
- Practice Guide, "Auditing Culture"

Risk and Control Effectiveness Reporting

The CAE is responsible for reporting on the overall effectiveness of the organization's internal control and risk management processes to both senior management and to the board. The CAE needs to form a holistic opinion regarding the general state of internal control in the organization, usually once each year.

To promote continuous improvement in maintaining effective controls, the internal audit activity typically provides the board and senior management with either:
- An overall assessment or
- Compiled results of control evaluations accumulated from individual audit engagements.

The CAE may recommend:
- The implementation of a control framework if one is not already in place.
- Actions that enhance the control environment (e.g., a "tone at the top" that promotes a culture of ethical behavior and a low tolerance for noncompliance).

Communication to senior management and the board regarding opinions on internal control and risk management processes needs to include:
- Information on the scope, scope limitations, and time period that the opinion pertains to.
- Whether other assurance providers or other projects were used to provide input.
- An executive summary of the opinion.
- Reference to the risk or control framework used to form the opinion.
- The overall opinion that was reached plus any reasons for an unfavorable opinion if there was one.

In an organization committed to governance and enterprise risk management, the ability of the board and senior management to provide oversight and to make sound decisions may be limited by various factors. For example, the board and senior management may not be familiar with the principles of risk management and how that should be affecting both oversight and business decisions.

The CAE can educate the board and senior management by:

- Reviewing the role of the board, senior management, operations, and internal auditing in the risk management process. This may be offered as a tutorial or a workshop during an annual meeting, or it can be required training for new board members and senior managers.

- Reviewing key, amended, and new laws, regulations, legal decisions, and standards that affect the organization's governance and operations. Periodically the CAE can include this review as an agenda item for a board/audit committee meeting.

- Facilitating workshops designed to identify emerging risks associated with the organization's business environment.

- Presenting at board/audit committee meetings on best practices in governance and risk management as practiced in peer organizations.

Topic D: Internal Audit Key Performance Indicators

This topic discusses the role that key performance indicators play in communicating the performance of the internal audit activity to senior management and the board, including some examples.

In addition to reviewing the contents of this topic, students can review the following IIA materials:
- Implementation Guidance for Standard 2060
- Implementation Guidance for Standard 1300
- Practice Guide, "Measuring Internal Audit Effectiveness and Efficiency"

Internal Audit KPI Reporting

In order to report on the internal audit activity's plans and the activity's performance relative to these plans, CAEs use key performance indicators, which are discussed more below.

To maintain and track consistent and effective communication with senior management and the board, the CAE may consider using a checklist of all other reporting requirements referenced throughout the *Standards*:

- Internal audit charter
  - According to Standard 1000, the internal audit activity's purpose, authority, and responsibility must be formally defined in the charter. The CAE must periodically review the charter and present it for approval to the board and senior management.
  - According to Standard 1010, the Mission of Internal Audit and the mandatory elements of the International Professional Practices Framework should also be discussed.

- Organizational independence of the internal audit activity
  - According to Standard 1110, the organizational independence of the internal audit activity must be confirmed to the board annually. Any interference in determining the scope of internal auditing, performing work, or communicating results—as well as the implications of such interference—must be disclosed to the board.
  - According to Standard 1111, the independent reporting relationship is essential to facilitate the CAE's ability to communicate directly with the board.

- Internal audit plans, resource requirements, and performance
  - Standard 2020 specifies the details of communicating the internal audit activity's plans and resource requirements. Standard 2060 adds the requirement to report the internal audit activity's performance relative to these plans.

- Results of audit engagements
  - The 2400 series of standards covers the requirements for communicating the results of audit engagements, including information that the engagement communications must contain, the quality of information, and the protocol in case of errors/omissions or nonconformance with the Code of Ethics or the *Standards* that affect a specific engagement.

- Quality assurance and improvement program
  - The 1300 series of standards covers the CAE's responsibility for developing and maintaining a quality assurance and improvement program that includes internal and external assessments.

- Conformance with the Code of Ethics and the *Standards*
  - Standard 1320 describes the details of reporting on the internal audit activity's conformance with the Code of Ethics and the *Standards*.
  - Standard 1322 describes considerations for reporting nonconformance.
  - Standard 2431 stipulates that information that must be disclosed when nonconformance impacts a specific engagement.

- Significant risk and control issues and management's acceptance of risk
  - This area is described by the 2100 series of standards, in addition to Standard 2060, discussed previously in this section.

Reports on any special requests made by the board or senior management may also be discussed during board meetings.

Most CAEs report on engagements in one of three ways:
- By providing a summary of audit work by area
- By discussing only major issues
- By distributing copies of all their audit reports

The goal should be to present a balanced, prioritized view of insights from audit work that enables the audit committee or board to perform its role.

Best practice reporting also provides:
- Executive summaries.
- Material in advance.
- Actions, not just issues.
- An event matrix.
- Nature, extent, and overall results of formal consulting engagements.

Demonstrating Conformance with Standard 2060

To demonstrate conformance with Standard 2060, the CAE may document discussions in agendas and minutes of meetings or in reports and presentations with attached distribution lists.

KPI Reporting

Care must be taken to identify appropriate performance measures—key performance indicators (KPIs) that are aligned to the organization's objectives and the internal audit charter and that target the performance necessary to meet activity objectives.

KPIs focus on accomplishments or behaviors that are valued by the organization. They are valid indicators of performance (i.e., they measure the right target) and are understandable to the internal audit staff who use them to guide and improve their performance.

KPIs measuring the internal audit activity itself are valuable because they allow the CAE to:
- Detect shortcomings in the activity.
- Plan remedial action.
- Demonstrate the value of internal auditing to customers.
- Support requests for resources needed to support the desired level of performance.

v7.0

Because of the close relationship between the internal auditing activity's KPIs and the expectations of the board and senior management, the CAE should establish KPIs that consider stakeholders' needs. In this way, the CAE can ensure that the activity's KPIs focus on meaningful performance that is aligned with the organization's strategic goals.

Occasionally, in-depth interviews and surveys should be conducted with stakeholders. The CAE should also consider periodically benchmarking the activity's KPIs against those of similar peer organizations.

Common KPIs for the internal audit activity include but are not limited to:
- Board (or audit committee) expectation met.
- Percentage of audit plan complete.
- Internal auditor workforce satisfaction.
- Client satisfaction goals—usefulness of recommendations.
- Cycle times (duration of period audits).
- Performance against the internal audit financial budget.
- Budget to actual audit times.
- Completion of initiatives in professional development plan.

The 1300 series of standards covers the CAE's responsibility for developing and maintaining a quality assurance and improvement program that includes internal and external assessments. The results of ongoing monitoring of the internal audit activity's performance should be reported in a manner desired by stakeholders at least annually. However, the CAE, board, and senior management may agree on more frequent reporting.

External assessment of the internal audit activity must be conducted at least once every five years, and the assessment must be discussed by the CAE with the board. This discussion must cover:
- The qualifications and independence of the external assessor or assessment team.
- Any potential conflict of interest.

The CAE should encourage board oversight of the external assessment.

Along with the annual report to senior management and the board regarding the results of ongoing monitoring, the CAE may include any recommendations for improvement.

Generally those assigned responsibility for conducting ongoing monitoring and periodic assessments communicate the results directly to the CAE while performing the assessments. In a smaller internal audit activity, the CAE may take a greater direct role in the internal assessment process. The results of internal assessments include, where appropriate:
- Corrective action plans.
- Progress against completion.

The CAE may distribute internal assessment reports to various stakeholders, including senior management, the board, and external auditors.

Section II: Planning the Engagement

This section is designed to help you:
- Establish engagement objectives/criteria.
- Differentiate engagement objectives from operational objectives.
- Identify the engagement scope.
- Define the scope limitations.
- Plan engagements to ensure identification of key risks and controls.
- Define a risk-based approach.
- Define internal controls that are considered likely to be relevant to the engagement.
- Complete a detailed risk assessment of each audit area.
- Use a risk control matrix to ensure that all significant risks are addressed in the audit.
- Define the benefits of a risk control matrix.
- Determine engagement procedures.
- Prepare an engagement work program.
- Describe the approval of the audit activity charter and plan.
- Define data collection.
- Identify various sources of evidence.
- Identify the types of audit tests.
- Determine the level of staff and resources needed for the engagement.
- Identify budget considerations.

 The IIA's guidance referenced in the Learning System may be accessed using the links below. Access to specific pages and documents varies for the public and The IIA members.
- **Attribute Standards:** www.theiia.org/Attribute-standards
- **Performance Standards:** www.theiia.org/Performance-standards
- **Standards and Guidance:** www.theiia.org/Guidance
- **Position Papers:** www.theiia.org/Position-papers
- **Implementation Guidance:** www.theiia.org/Practiceadvisories
- **Practice Guides and GTAGs:** www.theiia.org/Practiceguides

Section II moves from the general work of internal auditing to the specific processes used to plan engagements, which includes establishing engagement objectives, developing an audit program that incorporates activities aimed at meeting the organization's risk management objectives, and allocating staff and resources.

Chapter 1: Engagement Planning

Good engagement planning is essential in ensuring consistently successful internal audit engagements.

Topic A: Engagement Objectives, Criteria, and Scope

This topic discusses how to select engagement objectives, scope, and criteria, including key scope considerations and the main types of evaluation criteria.

In addition to reviewing the contents of this topic, students can review the following IIA materials:
- Implementation Guidance for Standard 2200
- Implementation Guidance for Standard 2210
- Implementation Guidance for Standard 2220
- Practice Guide, "Engagement Planning: Establishing Objectives and Scope"

Engagement Planning

The high-level requirements for engagement planning are covered by Standard 2200.

Performance Standard 2200, "Engagement Planning"

Internal auditors must develop and document a plan for each engagement, including the engagement's objectives, scope, timing, and resource allocations. The plan must consider the organization's strategies, objectives, and risks relevant to the engagement.

The *Standards* require four elements to be included in the actual plan, each covered by an individual standard:
- The objectives of the engagement
- The scope of the engagement
- The allocation of resources for the engagement
- The engagement work program

These four areas, along with evaluating risk and control factors, are discussed in this chapter.

Engagement Objectives

Performance Standard 2210, "Engagement Objectives"

Objectives must be established for each engagement.

Internal auditors must establish objectives as part of planning for each engagement. The IPPF glossary defines **engagement objectives** as "broad statements developed by internal

auditors that define intended engagement accomplishments." Internal audit engagement objectives should:
- Be aligned with related organizational objectives.
- Reflect the results of preliminary assessment of the risks relevant to the activity under review.

The main sources of information for preliminary objective development are:
- Review of internal audit plan.
- Review of prior engagement results.
- Discussions with stakeholders.
- Consideration of mission, vision, and objectives of the area or process under review.

When reviewing prior assessments, there are several sources the internal auditor may look to for information, as seen in Exhibit 2-4.

Exhibit 2-4: Prior Assessment Resources

Source	Information
Workpapers from previous audit engagements	These provide information about the processes and controls that were in place during the last review. They also enable internal auditors to inquire about any corrective actions taken by management to address previous internal audit observations.
Organization-wide risk assessments	These contain the risk priorities that the organization has identified to determine whether any of those risks should be included in the current engagement.
Fraud risk assessments	These contain fraud occurrences and investigated allegations in the area or process under review. Internal auditors should review relevant documentation to understand the facts from any allegation or investigation and the outcomes.
Reports by other assurance and consulting service providers	The work performed by other internal or external auditors or consulting service providers may allow auditors to avoid duplicating efforts. This is dependent on whether the internal auditor is satisfied that the work performed is relevant and reliable.

Interviews with relevant stakeholders help internal auditors better understand the objectives, design, operations, and control environment of the area or process under review. Examples of stakeholders and the information they may be able to provide are shown in Exhibit 2-5.

Exhibit 2-5: Interviewing Relevant Stakeholders

Stakeholders	Information Regarding Process Under Review
Personnel who perform the steps in a process	The personnel who perform the steps in a process are likely to provide unique information about how the process actually works, not just the way it was designed to operate. This can be especially valuable for identifying fraud risk.
Management	Management may be able to provide information documented in the form of policies, procedures, and self-assessments. Additional documentation may describe the area's business objectives and key performance indicators. Interviews may help internal auditors identify whether management's understanding of the steps in a process differs from that of the personnel who perform the steps.
IT personnel	IT personnel help ensure that all applicable systems are considered and may reveal points where controls might be missing, inadequate, or circumvented.
Legal counsel and compliance officers	Legal counsel and compliance officers may provide information received through whistleblower programs as well as information regarding unusual events and litigation relevant to the engagement. They may provide insight on how effectively compliance with existing polices and procedures satisfies laws and regulations.
Other stakeholders	Customers or other business areas that deal with the area or process under review may help the internal auditor understand past and/or current issues that could indicate potential risks.

Audit objectives often should be phrased in terms of contributing to the organization properly managing the activity's risks through effective governance, risk management, and control practices.

Engagement Objective Categories

Engagement objectives typically fall into three categories—operations, reporting, and compliance—which are aligned with the COSO internal control framework. These categories are at the top of the COSO internal framework cube, shown in Exhibit 2-6.

Exhibit 2-6: COSO Internal Control Framework Cube

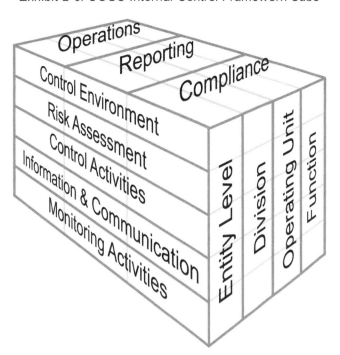

Operations objectives relate to how an entity strives to ensure that it can effectively and efficiently manage business operations. Reporting objectives relate to developing reliable financial and nonfinancial reports. Compliance objectives relate to determining that an entity is complying with applicable laws and regulations.

These categories are described further in Exhibit 2-7.

Exhibit 2-7: Broad Categories of Engagement Objectives

Category	Description
Operations	**Measures** such as: • Profitability (maximize revenue or minimize costs). • Delivery of excellent products and services. • Reduced processing time. • Safeguarding of assets (physical, human, information). • Support of organizational mission and vision. • Support of appropriate work environment for employees. **Examples:** • Evaluate if controls installed in systems are working to maximize the accuracy and efficiency of a process. • Evaluate controls over physical access to a facility. • Evaluate controls over safeguarding of assets. • Evaluate if the right personnel have been assigned the proper job responsibilities and have received appropriate training.

Category	Description
Reporting	**Measures** such as: • Maintenance of accurate financial records. • Collection of useful, reliable, and timely information for decision making. • External regulatory reporting. **Examples:** • Evaluate controls over timely recognition of revenues. • Evaluate if the identification and reporting of risks and controls are adequate for the enterprise risk management reporting process. • Identify and evaluate if the correct reports are given to the proper managers in the organization. • Validate the accuracy of reporting by confirming the accuracy of data provided. • Evaluate if the personnel responsible for reporting are providing accurate and timely reports.
Compliance	**Measures** such as: • Compliance with applicable laws and regulations. • Compliance with internal policies and procedures. **Examples:** • Evaluate the process in place to remain updated with legal and regulatory changes. • Evaluate how organizational compliance objectives and procedures are communicated to all employees. • Evaluate employee perception of the "tone at the top" in the business function being audited. • Evaluate controls in place to ensure that the travel expense policy is followed.

Here's an example of objectives that may be used in an accounts payable department.

Operating objective:	Pay invoices accurately and on a timely basis after verifying receipt of services or products.
Engagement objective:	Evaluate accurate and timely payment of invoices based on mitigation of risks, adequacy of controls, and compliance with financial policies and procedures.

Engagement Criteria

Implementation Standard 2210.A3 (Assurance Engagements)

Adequate criteria are needed to evaluate governance, risk management, and controls. Internal auditors must ascertain the extent to which management and/or the board has established adequate criteria to determine whether objectives and goals have been accomplished. If adequate, internal auditors must use such criteria in their evaluation. If inadequate, internal auditors must identify appropriate evaluation criteria through discussion with management and/or the board.

v7.0

Before an audit engagement can be performed, the lead auditor must identify the criteria to be used during the engagement. **Internal audit criteria** are the benchmarks against which the subject matter of the engagement can be assessed.

Adequate criteria are required to evaluate governance, risk management, and controls. Meaningful assurance can be provided to the board and senior management only if the conclusions reached are made in relation to suitable criteria.

Internal auditors can use criteria from management or the board if those criteria are adequate. Otherwise, the auditor must identify appropriate criteria through discussion with management and/or the board.

Three main types of criteria are:
- Internal (e.g., policies and procedures of the organization).
- External (e.g., laws and regulations imposed by statutory bodies).
- Leading practices (e.g., industry and professional guidance).

Scope of the Engagement

Performance Standard 2220, "Engagement Scope"

The established scope must be sufficient to achieve the objectives of the engagement.

Engagement procedures help the internal auditor to accomplish engagement objectives. Collectively, engagement objectives and procedures are what define the engagement scope. The scope helps delineate the boundaries of the engagement by identifying the activities being reviewed as well as any related activities that are not. It may also describe the nature and extent of audit work and provide additional supportive information.

For assurance engagements, audit scope and objectives are defined by the auditor. For consulting engagements, however, objectives and scope are defined collaboratively, by both the auditor and the engagement client.

The following are key considerations for setting scope:
- Boundaries of area or process
- In-scope versus out-of-scope locations
- Subprocesses
- Components of the area or process
- Time frame

Determining scope requires professional judgment based on relevant experience and/or supervisory assistance, as the *Standards* do not require that any specific areas be included in the scope for all types of engagements. However, the scope of assurance engagements falls under Standard 2220.A1.

Implementation Standard 2220.A1 (Assurance Engagements)

The scope of the engagement must include consideration of relevant systems, records, personnel, and physical properties, including those under the control of third parties.

The scope of consulting engagements is increasingly created using management input. Because of the emphasis in the *Standards* on auditor objectivity, this can be done without fear of compromising audit independence.

It is helpful to review engagement objectives to ensure that each one can be accomplished. A restriction placed on the internal audit activity that precludes it from accomplishing its objectives and plans for an engagement is typically referred to as a **scope limitation**. Among other things, a scope limitation may restrict:

- The scope defined in the charter.
- The internal audit activity's access to relevant records, personnel, and physical properties.
- The approved work schedule or level of effort.
- The performance of necessary engagement procedures.
- The approved staffing plan and financial budget of the audit function.

Recall the examples of objectives given earlier:

Operating objective:	Pay invoices accurately and on a timely basis after verifying receipt of services or products.
Engagement objective:	Evaluate accurate and timely payment of invoices based on mitigation of risks, adequacy of controls, and compliance with financial policies and procedures.

Based on these objectives, a scope statement should specify the following.

Inclusion:	What areas are within the scope (e.g., invoices, vendor management, accounts payable application, invoice processing, payments, accounting journal entries)?
Exclusion:	What are areas that a reasonable person would expect to find intentionally excluded from the scope?

A plausible scope statement example might be:

> The internal audit activity will conduct an operational assessment of the accounts payable department that will take into account all payments of invoices from January 1, 20xx, to December 31, 20xx.

Topic B: Engagement Planning Considerations

This topic discusses key considerations for auditors to ensure that engagements are planned correctly to achieve their goals.

In addition to reviewing the contents of this topic, students can review the following IIA materials:
- Implementation Guidance for Standard 2201
- Practice Guide, "Engagement Planning: Establishing Objectives and Scope"

Key Risks and Controls in Engagement Planning

Performance Standard 2201, "Planning Considerations"

In planning the engagement, internal auditors must consider:
- The strategies and objectives of the activity being reviewed and the means by which the activity controls its performance.
- The significant risks to the activity's objectives, resources, and operations and the means by which the potential impact of risk is kept to an acceptable level.
- The adequacy and effectiveness of the activity's governance, risk management, and control processes compared to a relevant framework or model.
- The opportunities for making significant improvements to the activity's governance, risk management, and control processes.

Auditors must identify the risks that may impact the objectives, resources, and/or operations of the area or process under review.

Auditors typically need to gather information on client policies. They seek to understand IT systems used as well as the sources, types, and reliability of information used in processes.

Additionally, internal auditors must determine whether new processes or conditions have introduced new risks.

Risk and Control Matrix

A risk and control matrix (also known as an engagement-level or audit risk assessment) is a useful tool to help ensure that internal auditors adequately account for risk at the engagement level and that all significant risks identified are addressed in subsequent fieldwork. No two matrices are exactly alike. An example is seen in Exhibit 2-8. Risk and control matrices are discussed further in the context of evaluating the effectiveness of control systems in Part 1.

Exhibit 2-8: Sample Risk and Control Matrix

Business Objective	Inherent Risk	Impact (L, M, H)	Likelihood (L, M, H)	Control

Source: Adapted from Practice Guide, "Engagement Planning: Establishing Objectives and Scope."

A risk and control matrix can be time-consuming to develop. But the benefits of using the tool are significant. In addition to generally helping to account for risk at the engagement level and identify all significant risks, developing a matrix during the planning phase:

- Sets the stage for a more effective and efficient audit by focusing the audit on the areas of greatest risk.
- Ties the audit together by documenting the complete thought process from risk identification to audit program development.
- "Teaches" the risk assessment thought process; area management becomes a more effective "owner" of control.
- Facilitates participatory auditing.

Many organizations use the risk and control matrix as a way to develop a list of all the controls to be tested during the internal audit. By including this level of detail, the matrix can also serve as the work/audit program for the engagement. Further, incorporating testing results can make the risk and control matrix the major workpaper for each area of the engagement.

Topic C: Detailed Risk Assessments

This topic discusses how to complete and use a detailed risk assessment when performing engagement planning.

In addition to reviewing the contents of this topic, students can review the following IIA materials:
- Practice Guide, "Engagement Planning: Assessing Fraud Risks"
- Practice Guide, "Engagement Planning: Establishing Objectives and Scope"

Evaluating Risk and Control Factors

Internal auditors must conduct a preliminary assessment of risks relevant to the activity under review. The preliminary risk assessment ensures that the engagement is targeted at risk related to the topic of the specific internal audit engagement. Objectives must reflect the results of the risk assessment, and other significant areas of concern can be identified based on the risk assessment as well.

By building the foundation of the engagement on a risk assessment, auditors can focus on relevant risks and provide value to the organization.

Objectives are not necessarily limited to the risks identified in the overall risk assessment, however, as evidenced by Standard 2210.A2.

Implementation Standard 2210.A2 (Assurance Engagements)

Internal auditors must consider the probability of significant errors, fraud, noncompliance, and other exposures when developing the engagement objectives.

Overall risk assessments are not expected to identify every risk or weakness that needs to be considered at the engagement level. As the engagement progresses beyond the planning stage, auditors are still responsible for being alert to signs of risk.

For example, when doing a preliminary assessment of risks associated with fraud for an area, the internal auditor may look for the following red flags:

- Management issues
  - Lack of area expertise
  - Lack of supervision
  - History of legal violations

- Personnel issues
  - Lack of background checks
  - Dissatisfied employees
  - Unwillingness to share duties

- Process issues
  - Duties not segregated
  - Poor physical security
  - Poor access controls

v7.0

Risk-Based Approach

A risk-based approach requires internal auditors to first understand the entity and its environment in order to identify risks. An experienced auditor's skill and judgment is exercised to put the focus on the specific information that should be obtained through this process. This reduces the potential for unnecessary information or information overload, saving critical time and resources.

Understanding the entity involves documenting:
- Operational objectives or goals.
- Level of compliance with laws, policies, and procedures.
- Key processes.
- Organizational structure (e.g., reporting relationships and supervision).
- Information systems.
- Identified key risks.
- Current controls.

Gathering this information can be done in many ways, including:
- Initial client meetings.
- Conducting a preliminary survey.
- Performing analytical review procedures.
- Conducting interviews.
- Observation.
- Inspection of processes and documentation.
- Benchmarking.
- Reviewing prior internal audit reports and those of other assurance providers.

By assessing identified risks, several factors (such as the nature of the risks, relevant controls, and level of evidence) are taken into consideration. The result of a risk assessment categorizes the engagement into areas of significant risk and areas of normal risk.

Topic D: Engagement Procedures and Work Program

This topic discusses how an auditor decides which engagement procedures to use and how to create and use an engagement work program.

In addition to reviewing the contents of this topic, students can review the following IIA materials:
- Implementation Guidance for Standard 2240

Preparing the Engagement Work Program

Performance Standard 2240, "Engagement Work Program"

Internal auditors must develop and document work programs that achieve the engagement objectives.

Implementation Standard 2240.A1 (Assurance Engagements)

Work programs must include the procedures for identifying, analyzing, evaluating, and documenting information during the engagement. The work program must be approved prior to its implementation, and any adjustments approved promptly.

The IPPF glossary defines an **engagement work program** as "a document that lists the procedures to be followed during an engagement, designed to achieve the engagement plan." An engagement work program is also called an audit program during assurance engagements; thus, the two terms are often interchanged.

Prior to developing the work program, auditors may need to consider:
- Appropriate sample size for testing and methodologies used.
- Risk register or risk matrix and how it applies to the development of the work program.
- Scope of the engagement.
- How the engagement objectives will be achieved.
- Whether necessary resources are available.
- Judgments and conclusions made during the engagement's planning phase.

Internal auditors must determine which tests or audit steps are necessary to assess the risks in the area or process under review and which to use in testing the existing controls. The auditor must ensure that the tests are specific enough to avoid scope creep.

A well-crafted engagement work program:
- Starts with clearly specifying the engagement work and audit program objectives.
- Provides an outline of work to be performed and facilitates an understanding of the audited area.
- Furnishes evidence that the work is adequately planned.
- Provides a record for audit management review.
- Provides assurances that all significant risks have received adequate consideration.
- Assists in controlling work and assignment responsibilities.
- Gives order and coherence to the audit.
- Addresses the need for conclusions responsive to audit objectives.

The format of the work program may vary by engagement or organization, but it must be approved by internal audit management prior to commencement of audit fieldwork.

An engagement work program becomes guidance for performing the engagement. A sample work program is shown in Exhibit 2-9.

Exhibit 2-9: Work Program Example

Audit Objectives:

Obj. 1	To determine that a preventive maintenance schedule has been developed and adhered to so that vehicles are safe and drivable.
Obj. 2	To determine that the authorized vendor lists and contracts are current and based on company standards so that external maintenance and repairs are performed by qualified vendors.
Obj. 3	To determine that a repair log of in-house and vendor repairs is properly prepared so that maintenance is performed and documented according to company standards.
Obj. 4	To determine that the policy governing in-house repairs is followed so that minor mechanical repairs are made in-house.
Obj. 5	To determine that vendor price lists are current, so that cars are repaired by authorized vendors at reasonable rates.
Obj. 6	To determine that supporting documentation exists and that expenses can be properly monitored and verified for reasonableness.
Obj. 7	To determine that maintenance expenses are properly recorded in the general ledger and are monitored.

Test Step	WP Reference	Initial/ Date

1. Obtain preventive maintenance schedule, a cars inventory listing at 12/31/xx, and a report of car additions and deletions for the audit period.
  A. Verify that all cars owned during the audit period are on the schedule. (Compare preventive maintenance schedule to inventory records, reports.)
  B. Attest to the completeness of the schedule. Determine that the schedule contains the VEHNO, VIN, car description, scheduled maintenance dates, actual maintenance dates, and a description of the procedures performed. Document any exceptions and perform follow-up procedures.		

2. Select 30 cars from the preventive maintenance schedule for the audit period and test for the following attributes:
  A. Preventive maintenance was performed and documented on schedule in accordance with company policy (belts, hoses, fluids, brakes checked...).
  B. Preventive maintenance was performed within established time frames or mileage parameters.
  C. Mechanic's record was obtained on preventive maintenance schedule repairs to be performed by outside vendors. Trace repair to repair log, vendor invoice, and bank's payment receipt confirmation.
  D. Mechanics initialed and dated preventive maintenance schedule.
  E. Evidence obtained of supervisory review.		

3. Obtain vendor contracts; review for propriety and reasonableness. Determine that contracts are current and in agreement with the authorized vendor list.		

4. Obtain repair log for the audit period.
  A. Determine that work performed on cars is documented on the repair log and performed by approved vendors.
  B. Examine repair log and determine that work performed by outside vendors is in line with company policy. (Work that can be performed in-house should not be performed by outside vendors.)		

5. Select 30 repairs from the repair log during the audit period and test for the following attributes:
  A. Proper completion of the repair log.
  B. Repair work performed by a vendor is adequately described.
  C. Mechanics initialed and dated repair log.
  D. Evidence of supervisory review.
  E. Trace repair to service request form and invoice.
  F. Repairs performed by authorized vendors. Trace to authorized vendor list.
  G. If in-house repair, ascertain that current policy authorizes in-house repair.		

6. Obtain current price lists for vendor repairs. Compare to an industry auto parts and service guide to determine reasonableness of prices.		

Source: "Auditing Techniques" course, The Institute of Internal Auditors, 2006 (abridged).

v7.0

Note that an actual work program would contain additional steps to achieve the audit objectives. The final steps would be addressing identified potential risk/control issues with management and adding a concluding statement responsive to audit program objectives.

Keep in mind that each work program will be unique, depending on the scope of the engagement, as evidenced by Standard 2240.C1.

Implementation Standard 2240.C1 (Consulting Engagements)

Work programs for consulting engagements may vary in form and content depending upon the nature of the engagement.

Determine Engagement Procedures

Each engagement procedure should be designed to test a particular control that addresses risk. A procedure may be applicable to the internal audit as a whole, but if it is applied erroneously to an objective, the result will be irrelevant.

There is no definitive list of internal audit procedures or a road map for matching procedures to engagement objectives. The internal auditor needs to discriminate between procedures that may be relevant and those that are unimportant.

Other attributes of good procedures include accurate, reliable, timely, reasonable, and complete.

Topic E: Engagement Resources

This topic discusses how auditors ensure that they have appropriate and sufficient resources to accomplish an engagement and what should be done if required resources are not available.

In addition to reviewing the contents of this topic, students can review the following IIA materials:
• Implementation Guidance for Standard 2230

Staff Levels

Performance Standard 2230, "Engagement Resource Allocation"

Internal auditors must determine appropriate and sufficient resources to achieve engagement objectives based on an evaluation of the nature and complexity of each engagement, time constraints, and available resources.

v7.0

In terms of staff, "appropriate resources" refers to the mix of knowledge, skills, and other competencies needed to perform the engagement.

In determining the level of audit staff for an engagement, the audit leader should consider:

- **The objectives of the audit and their implications in terms of necessary skills and knowledge**. Team leaders should consider the need for "soft" skills as well, especially in audits of sensitive areas such as governance. Well-known and respected staff members may be needed to staff these engagements.

- **The availability of staff with the necessary knowledge and skills**. Specialized skill sets can be invaluable if used properly. If the skills of available auditors are not sufficient, consider whether additional training is an option or whether closer supervision is appropriate.

- **The nature of the audit's deadline**. This may be a concern if a report is needed for compliance reasons or due diligence. It may be necessary to complete this audit in order to proceed to a related audit area.

- **The activity's priorities and resources**. Some resources may be necessary for audits considered to have a higher priority in the audit plan.

A decision may be made that additional knowledge, skills, and competencies are needed to perform the engagement. External services may need to be obtained to support or complement the internal audit team. Information technology is an example of an area that often requires external expertise.

Required Resources

To determine how to best allocate resources, auditors should understand the engagement:
- Objectives.
- Scope.
- Nature.
- Complexity.

The success of an engagement is often judged by:
- Achievement to the level of standards.
- Fulfillment of engagement objectives.
- Completion within budget.

Setting a budget is an important consideration in engagement planning. It is often the principal control over the audit engagement.

Engagement budgets include statements of the time allocated, as time is the key factor in an internal audit activity. Budgeted hours (or time budgets) must be realistic and achievable. Some internal audit activities use deadlines to manage their budgets, often based on the level of associated risk.

Factors that may impact a time budget include:
- The collective skills and expertise of the internal audit team.
- Logistics, such as client availability, site locations, and travel time.
- Available technology that is helpful or necessary to perform the engagement.

There are different schools of thought about the execution of time budgets:
- Adhere to the defined number of hours and move from the work once the time is expired.
- Perform engagement responsibilities to the fullest extent, even if this means that budgeted hours are exceeded.
- If necessary, add staff and possibly monetary resources to perform the work within the scheduled time.

It is always best that time budgets be sufficiently flexible to cover unanticipated demands on the internal audit activity. While time demands might require reducing scope or quality on recurring audits of lower risk, time demands should not be allowed to impact work quality in higher-risk areas.

Section III: Performing the Engagement

This section is designed to help you:
- Perform a preliminary survey of the engagement area, starting with a review of previous audit reports and other relevant documentation.
- Show how checklists/internal control questionnaires, interviews, walkthroughs, and observation can be effectively employed in gathering audit information.
- Describe various sampling methods and the purpose of each method.
- Describe commonly used statistical and judgmental (nonstatistical) sampling techniques.
- Demonstrate the use of flowcharts to aid in process mapping.
- Identify and evaluate various types of audit data and gather the best type to support audit findings.
- Evaluate the relevance, sufficiency, and reliability of audit evidence.
- Explore available computer software packages used, for example, in continuous auditing, data extraction, spreadsheet analysis, and workpaper automation.
- Apply analytical review techniques such as testing for reasonableness, performing ratio analysis, analyzing variances, detecting trends, or performing regression analysis.
- Draw conclusions from data analysis efforts.
- Develop and review clear, comprehensive documentation/workpapers to support audit conclusions and recommendations.
- Communicate test results and interim conclusions regarding controls in a professional manner to the auditor-in-charge to ensure that they receive a full hearing.
- Base sound conclusions and persuasive recommendations upon well-researched and logically organized audit findings.
- Direct/supervise individual engagements.
- Create an audit work plan.
- Nurture instrumental relationships, build bonds, and work toward shared goals.
- Coordinate work assignments among audit team members when serving as auditor-in-charge of a project.
- Complete performance appraisals of engagement staff.

The IIA's guidance referenced in the Learning System may be accessed using the links below. Access to specific pages and documents varies for the public and The IIA members.
- **Attribute Standards:** www.theiia.org/Attribute-standards
- **Performance Standards:** www.theiia.org/Performance-standards
- **Standards and Guidance:** www.theiia.org/Guidance
- **Position Papers:** www.theiia.org/Position-papers
- **Implementation Guidance:** www.theiia.org/Practiceadvisories
- **Practice Guides and GTAGs:** www.theiia.org/Practiceguides

Chapter 1: Information Gathering

This chapter describes the inputs gathered during both the preliminary survey and the course of the engagement.

As with any process, the quality of inputs is directly related to the quality of outputs—in this case, the output of reliable conclusions and recommendations. When attempting to determine what types and amounts of data will be sufficient and appropriate, it is important to begin with the end in mind. First determine the objectives of the engagement, and then work to find the proper sources of information to fulfill those objectives.

Topic A: Preliminary Survey Information Gathering and Examination

This topic discusses how and where auditors can find relevant information at the start of an engagement.

In addition to reviewing the contents of this topic, students can review the following IIA materials:
- Implementation Guidance for Standard 2300
- Implementation Guidance for Standard 2310
- Implementation Guidance for Standard 2320

Engagement Area Surveys

Performance Standard 2300, "Performing the Engagement"

Internal auditors must identify, analyze, evaluate, and document sufficient information to achieve the engagement's objectives.

Because of the non-sequential nature of required portions of audit engagements, when preparing to perform an engagement, auditors should review standards representing:
- Planning (2200 series).
- Performing and supervising (2300 series).
- Communicating (2400 series).

v7.0

Information formulated during the planning process should include:

- Engagement objectives that reflect the results of a preliminary risk assessment (Standard 2210/2210.A1).
- Criteria that will be used to evaluate the governance, risk management, and controls of the area or process under review (Standard 2210.A3).
- The engagement work program (Standard 2240/2240.A1).

Work performed during the planning phase is documented in workpapers and referenced during the work program and may include:

- A risk and control matrix.
- Process maps, flowcharts, and/or narrative descriptions of control processes.
- The results of evaluating the adequacy of control design.
- A plan and approach for testing the effectiveness of key controls.

The level and analysis of detail applied, as well as the timing of step completion, varies by internal audit activity and engagement.

Internal auditors:

- Should approach engagements with an objective and inquisitive mind and search strategically for information.
- Must apply professional skepticism to evaluate whether:
  - The information is sufficient and appropriate to provide a reasonable basis on which to form conclusions or recommendations.
  - Additional information is needed.

Standard 2330 requires that internal auditors document information resulting from the execution of the engagement and that the evidence should logically support the conclusions and engagement results.

Sufficient information is factual, adequate, and convincing so that a prudent, informed person would reach the same conclusions as the auditor.

Performance Standard 2320, "Analysis and Evaluation"

Internal auditors must base conclusions and engagement results on appropriate analyses and evaluation.

Per Standard 2320, the ultimate goal of assurance engagements and some consulting engagements might be to reach conclusions about whether the design and operation of key controls support the engagement subject's ability to achieve its objectives. The results of the analysis and evaluation process may be added to the risk control matrix, if one was created during the engagement planning phase.

Internal auditors usually create a testing plan to gather evidence about the operating effectiveness of adequately designed key controls.

- Generally, secondary controls and controls that have a design weakness do not need to be tested.
- Controls that have a design weakness do need to be documented and reported.
- If the details of the testing plan are not sufficient, auditors may need to provide additional testing details.

The approach to evaluation often includes a combination of manual audit procedures and computer-assisted auditing techniques (CAATs).

Manual audit procedures include:
- Inquiry.
- Inspection.
- Observation.
- Vouching.
- Tracing.
- Reperformance.
- Confirmation.
- Analytical procedures.

CAATs include:
- Generalized audit software programs.
- Specialized programs that test processing logic and controls of other software and systems.
- Data analytics.

Conformance can be demonstrated by engagement workpapers that describe the actions, analyses, and evaluations performed during an engagement as well as the logic supporting the conclusions, opinions, and/or advice.

Previous Audit Documentation

Internal auditors can learn a great deal from reviewing audit-related documentation, including but not limited to prior audit reports and data.

The internal auditor should begin by looking at prior audit documentation that is relevant. This may be found in a permanent file. (A permanent file is a record of consistent, rarely changing documents.) Such documentation of prior audits can include:
- Workpapers.
- Findings.
- Reports.
- Replies.

- Auditor comments.
- Contracts.
- Related information.

It is usually appropriate to review the work of other internal or external assurance activities that were performed for the activity or are in process. This may include:
- The work of external auditors.
- External management letters.
- Other third-party reports such as an internal compliance review.
- The results of an external regulatory examination.

Note that, in general, evidence obtained from third-party sources is considered more reliable than evidence obtained from audit client personnel because the internal auditor receives it directly from independent sources. "Confirmation" is the term used to describe obtaining direct written verification of the accuracy of information from independent third parties, and it may be positive or negative.
- Positive confirmation asks recipients to respond regardless of whether or not they believe the information is correct.
- Negative confirmation asks recipients to respond only when they believe the information is incorrect.

Audit activity monitoring reports can also be reviewed to understand the status of any open issues identified in previous internal audits of the area. An important item to check when reviewing previous audit reports is whether all prior audit issues have been adequately included in ongoing follow-up procedures, such as by being included in management's tracking process, or if the issues have already been resolved.

Additional documents that are typically appropriate for review include relevant:
- Organizational information (e.g., organizational charts, number and names of employees, key employees).
- Details about recent changes in the organization, including major system changes.
- Job descriptions.
- Statements of authority and responsibility for the area.
- Objectives and goals.
- Procedural manuals, instructions, and directives.
- Project plans.
- Physical reports.
- Performance reports.
- Certificates of compliance.
- Schedules for production, projects, personnel, etc.
- Budget information, operating results, and financial data on the activity to be reviewed.
- Correspondence files to determine potential significant engagement issues.

- Input for the organization's enterprise risk management evaluations.
- Board and committee terms of reference and minutes for relevant governance activities.
- Internet and intranet sites relevant to the area being audited.
- Public documents produced by the area being audited, such as brochures, reports, plans, posters, advertisements, and instructions.

Another valuable activity is to research and review authoritative and technical literature appropriate to the activity, such as:
- Internal auditing literature.
- Industry practices and methods.
- Trade practices.

This is particularly beneficial if the engagement is a first-time audit or is in response to an emerging risk.

Documentation can be in any format, for example, paper, audio, or video. Increasingly, internal auditors can access information electronically from remote locations. This capability allows much of the review process to be completed before the internal auditor arrives at the engagement site. If hard-copy documentation or tangible materials must be reviewed at a specific location, they should never be removed. As necessary, copies can be made.

The review of prior audit documentation is important because it:
- Provides familiarity with the area to be audited.
- Overviews what to expect in the activity being audited.
- Shows how other auditors approached the assignment.
- Identifies specific problems found previously and areas likely to have continuing or repeat problems (e.g., high-risk or repeat findings).
- Reveals the status of promises or actions taken to correct any nonconformance.
- Reveals strengths that were previously identified that should be verified to ensure that they have been sustained.
- May identify additional activities for evaluation during the audit.

Study of previous audit files and records does not necessarily mean that the same approach can be used for the upcoming audit. An internal auditor needs to evaluate any changes since the prior audit in:
- Organizational goals and objectives.
- The client operation.
- Risks.
- The internal audit activity.
- New technologies and any other mitigating factors that can influence the current engagement.

Even if circumstances differ, prior engagement documentation still provides a step forward in the planning process.

After reviewing prior audit documentation, internal auditors must retain their focus on the current audit. While these reviews should provide good information, results and conclusions must be determined during the activity of the current audit.

Walkthroughs

Walkthroughs are step-by-step demonstrations or explanations of a process or task conducted by the process or task owner in the presence of the internal auditor. Internal auditors can use walkthroughs to better understand a process flow. Walkthroughs can also be used to verify the actual state of controls in an organization—that is, which controls are included in normal activities because they are efficient and effective to execute in the real world and which are omitted, altered, or erroneously executed some or all of the time.

Exhibit 2-10 shows that walkthroughs can help reveal the root cause of a control weakness or failure.

Exhibit 2-10: What Walkthroughs May Reveal

Walkthrough Reveals . . .	Potential Root Cause(s)	Potential Recommendation
The employee is not executing the control.	The employee has an incomplete understanding of the control procedure or its purpose.	Recommend better training on the control.
	The employee is deliberately omitting the control due to time, cost, or other motives.	Report the issue to local management.
The employee performs the control correctly despite evidence of control failures.	The employee does not usually perform the control and is doing it only when observed.	Discuss the potential problem with local management.
The employee is attempting to execute the control but is not following the proper procedure.	The employee has an incomplete understanding of the procedure or is deliberately modifying it.	Implement better training or management discipline.
	The procedure does not work well in practice despite being theoretically sound, either because the environment has changed since the procedure was designed or because the process owner had no input in control design and it is impractical to implement as written.	Recommend that the control be revised or redesigned with process owner input to be more effective and/or efficient.

Separating failures in the design of controls from failures in their execution can help internal auditors add value.

Observations

To the auditor, **observation** implies a stricter discipline than ordinary "looking around." The more knowledge, experience, and skill an auditor acquires, the better able he or she is to gather significant audit information through purposeful visual examination of, among other things:

• People.
• Activities.
• Facilities.
• Inventories.
• Safety systems.
• Office layouts.
• Equipment.

Observation can take many forms, including walkthroughs. In some types of audits, observations made and recorded by a camera make up a significant portion of testing. These photographs or videos may become the audit findings for documentation and reporting. This approach is particularly appropriate for environmental and health and safety audits.

Observations gain significance when the auditor puts them into context, which is best accomplished when they know what to look for before beginning to make observations. This may mean mentally comparing an observed fact to:

• Past observations.
• Claims made by the audit client.
• Industry standards.
• Regulations.

Disciplined observation notices what is missing as well as what is present: the lack of necessary safety devices, the absence of a necessary inspector, equipment present but not in use.

Observations, by themselves, generally constitute weak evidence. To gain force in an audit report, observations may need to be backed up by other evidence and analysis that confirms what the auditor has seen. In some instances, having the client participate in the observations and agree to the findings—such as by performing a walkthrough—helps to confirm the observation. If this is not possible, the report should identify the observed information as such.

While observation yields insights, it can also provide misleading data if not done carefully and cross-checked with other methods. Being observed may very well cause people on the job to behave differently. Nevertheless, observation can add a valuable perspective to complement other information.

Interviews

The auditor also gathers information directly from internal and external persons. The quality of this information depends upon the skillful use of tools such as interviews.

An **interview** is generally described as a structured discussion in which a person is asked questions about his or her opinions, activities, and other areas of interest. An audit interview occupies a middle ground between a polite conversation and an interrogation. Like a conversation, an interview should be pleasant and relaxed. Unlike an ordinary conversation, however, the audit interview has (or should have) a formal structure, which the auditor provides. The audit interview may involve a certain amount of risk for the person answering the auditor's questions, so the auditor needs to develop considerable skill in putting people at ease.

Interviews can be in person, video-based, or via telephone. Face-to-face interviews are preferable, but not every situation lends itself to that format.

During the engagement planning process, interviews are often conducted to:
- Secure the perspective of management responsible for the activity being examined.
- Clarify information about the area to be audited.
- Collect additional necessary information.
- Provide an observation of the activities in the organization to be audited.

Topic B: Checklists and Questionnaires

This topic discusses how auditors can create and use checklists and risk and control questionnaires as part of the engagement and how the CAE can standardize portions of these tools for increased efficiency in the internal audit activity.

Checklists and Questionnaires

The internal audit function can use a risk assessment survey to get input from middle management. It may be brief and open ended, or it may be a structured survey asking managers to assess a number of risk categories or risk-related statements. If HR or an outside vendor administers an entity-wide survey asking employees to evaluate elements of the work environment, this may also be a valuable source of risk assessment information.

Checklists

A **checklist** is a simple visual tool used to collect, track, and analyze data. It allows the internal auditor to work in an organized and efficient manner. Checklists are developed during the planning phase, typically at the end of the preliminary survey.

A checklist includes items and boxes or spaces for a checkmark to indicate whether the item is present.
- A checkmark indicates that the item is present.
- A blank checkbox indicates that the item is not present.
- Space to record notes, evidence, references, and comments may also be included in the checklist.

A checklist has several uses:
- As a reminder device that helps the auditor be certain that he or she has asked all the questions or made all the observations intended
- As a quick method of gathering information from a respondent
- As a control to be sure that all the correct activities are being performed to complete the audit with correct and accurate information

When checklists are used as reminders, they are also useful for tracking activities from the beginning to the end of an audit engagement. In practice, they have critical significance in planning an engagement:
- They can be used to support important administrative tasks such as travel arrangements (travel time, hotels, etc.) and system access.
- They help to establish consistency throughout the audit team and ensure that the members of the team follow work schedules for testing, reporting results to the auditor-in-charge or client management, completing workpapers, and performing other tasks.
- They help to ensure that the internal audit activity addresses all the appropriate areas and collects data for each when performing the audit.

Ultimately, checklists guide the internal audit activity and help fulfill the scope of the audit engagement.

Questionnaires

A **questionnaire** is a tool for documenting information gathered across multiple survey participants. Internal auditors also use questionnaires during preliminary surveys and in control self-assessments.

When using a questionnaire for any of these purposes, the internal auditor should consider the most effective way to frame the questions and organize the responses. Examples of how questions may be framed include allowing respondents to:

- Answer questions by marking predetermined answers, such as yes or no.
- Give narratives of limited or unlimited length.
- Respond to given statements using rating scales. Scales can:
  - Be numerical (1 to 5, 1 to 10, etc.).
  - Use words to describe categories (always, sometimes, never; strongly agree, agree, no opinion, disagree, strongly disagree; etc.).

Choosing the proper format for questions and responses can make the difference between useful and useless information.

Some participants will refuse to respond to questionnaires of any sort, fearing the consequences of providing their opinion in writing on a particular topic. Sometimes respondents will provide positive answers whether they have positive feelings or not, simply to shorten the audit.

Because of their limitations, questionnaires are best used in gathering information about:

- Multiple units, such as branches, that have the same processes, risks, and standard operating procedures. In such situations, questionnaires provide uniform information for use in comparisons.
- Regulatory compliance or other yes/no matters.

Yes/No Questionnaires

Yes/no questionnaires allow only a simple yes or no response. (In essence, checklists, which were described above, are compact yes/no questionnaires.) This type of questionnaire is suitable for only some purposes and not for others (depending in part upon the format).

Some general advantages of yes/no questionnaires are:

- They are easy to administer.
- They yield uniform information from all informants for accurate comparisons.
- They can be given to large numbers of informants and to informants in different branches, countries, etc.
- The results of large response pools can be aggregated and analyzed easily.

Among their disadvantages, questionnaires of the yes/no variety:

- Are not appropriate for all types of situations or issues.
- Are not suited to gathering in-depth knowledge.
- Reduce the auditor's chance to observe the respondent's behavior and environment.

Internal Control Questionnaires (ICQs)

An **internal control questionnaire (ICQ)** is a preconstructed array of questions used to elicit key information about internal controls, especially when documenting initial responses to questions about these controls. Such questionnaires are sometimes referred to as "predesigned surveys." They allow for efficient gathering of information from large numbers of respondents at one time but do not allow for follow-up questions and observation of audit customer behavioral cues.

ICQs start with a known or desired answer (a yes or no response) and then seek specific comments. In this regard, the basic structure of an ICQ differs from open-ended questionnaires, which are used to solicit only narrative responses. ICQs may be used in different business areas to answer various control-related questions. ICQs may be completed by the auditor, as depicted below, or completed directly by the process owners.

Exhibit 2-11 shows an excerpt of an ICQ for an accounts payable disbursement process. The internal auditor or client records comments in the space provided. Observing the event is better than asking the client (the inquiry method) or having the client directly enter comments but not as desirable as examining evidence obtained through testing.

Exhibit 2-11: Sample ICQ for a Disbursement Process

Question	Answer	Comments	Method Used	Performed By
Are disbursements over $136,000 sent by wire and disbursements below this amount sent by ACH?	Yes ☑ No ☐	*Separate personnel perform disbursements via wire versus ACH based on this monetary cutoff guide.*	Inquire ☐ Observe ☑ Test ☐	Initials: *IPS*
Does the company review the ACH positive pay exception file from the bank and provide decisions to the bank prior to the 2:00 p.m. deadline each day?	Yes ☑ No ☐	*ACH disbursements specialists get few exceptions and review them promptly to avoid the default "pay none" option.*	Inquire ☑ Observe ☐ Test ☐	Initials: *JCK and RDM*

ICQs are efficient and easy to administer. Essentially, they provide a checklist to help with further evaluation after an initial risk assessment. Good applications for ICQs are across multiple units with the same processes, risks, and expected controls. Basic constraints in using ICQs include that they:

- Are limited to questions with yes/no answers about procedures.
- Do not provide for in-depth investigation.

An important assumption in using an ICQ is that the internal auditor knows what the procedures should be. Ongoing review helps to ensure that the questions asked and the information collected remain relevant. Many of these questions may identify activities to be tested during the audit fieldwork.

Topic C: Sampling and Statistical Analysis

This topic discusses the differences in sampling and statistical analysis techniques and how some of the major methods can be employed by auditors when conducting engagements, based on the characteristics of the particular engagement.

Sampling and Statistical Analysis

Audit sampling is commonly used to test the operating effectiveness of controls. Increasingly, auditors can apply analysis to a large population of data to identify anomalies.

The four Vs of data (volume, velocity, variety, and veracity) enable auditors to take advantage of the possibilities of data analytics. Auditors using data analytics must be well versed in each of these attributes.

Auditors must select the proper quantity of instances (such as transactions, as an example) to test in order to determine whether controls are consistently operating as designed, with an acceptable level of exceptions. Auditors must determine how representative of the entire population the sample needs to be. This determination will guide the decision on sampling method and sample size.

Two general approaches to audit sampling are statistical and nonstatistical (or judgmental). The decision on which approach to use considers both cost and quality. Statistical sampling allows the auditor to quantify, measure, and control sampling risk, but it may be costlier, depending on which nonstatistical technique it is being compared to.

Statistical Sampling

Statistical sampling methods provide:

- An objective basis for determining sample sizes and/or for randomly selecting sample items (units) for testing.
- A methodology for projecting sample results to the population (i.e., the likely number of errors or exceptions that would be found if all items were tested).

These projections are compared to the thresholds that differentiate acceptable from unacceptable numbers of exceptions or errors.

Management may set standards for maximum error rates for their own purposes, and this information can be used to help set these levels, but internal auditors may perceive the level of risk from an assurance coverage perspective as requiring a tighter standard than management has established.

Statistical Sampling Techniques

Attributes sampling is a statistical technique that has a number of variations, including stratified random sampling, stop-and-go sampling, and discovery sampling.

Attributes Sampling

Attributes sampling approaches enable the user to reach a conclusion about a population in terms of rate of occurrence. It is called for when the audit objective is to estimate the number of times a certain characteristic occurs in a population without regard to the size of the characteristic (i.e., the characteristic exists or does not exist; an error occurs or does not occur).

Attributes sampling involves nine steps:
1. Identify a specific internal control objective and the prescribed controls aimed at achieving that objective.
2. Define what is meant by a control deviation.
3. Define the population and sampling unit.
4. Determine the appropriate values of the parameters affecting sample size.
5. Determine the appropriate sample size.
6. Randomly select the sample.
7. Audit the sample items selected and count the number of deviations from the prescribed control.
8. Determine the achieved upper deviation limit.
9. Evaluate the sample results.

Stratified Random Sampling

Sometimes a population contains such wide variation that it must be subdivided into more coherent units before selecting random samples. In stratified random sampling, a population is divided into strata with distinct characteristics. Although software exists to aid in stratification, the auditor's judgment is usually a reliable guide. For example, perhaps there is a category of spending that is within a manager's discretion, followed by one or more categories requiring a higher level of authorization. Stratified random sampling could be used to separately evaluate each category, since each has different controls and risks.

Stop-and-Go Sampling

To avoid testing an unnecessarily large number of items when doing attributes sampling, auditors have developed the stop-and-go method. Stop-and-go sampling applies to situations in which the auditor suspects the population to be relatively error-free.

The auditor determines the error rate in a small sample and then:
- If the sample demonstrates the anticipated low error rate, the auditor may stop sampling.
- If the error rate turns out to be larger than expected, the auditor will go ahead with further sampling.

This might require one or a succession of small samples that either confirm the original view of the population or continue to indicate the existence of a higher-than-expected error rate. In the latter instance, the auditor may consider reverting to full-scale statistical sampling to determine the actual error rate at a desired confidence level and precision.

Tables are available to help the auditor evaluate the results of small stop-and-go samples. If the auditor uses a sample of 25 items from a total population of 10,000, a table could provide information correlating various numbers of errors in the sample with the likelihood of various error rates in the population.

Discovery Sampling

Unlike other attributes sampling methods, discovery sampling does not intend to characterize a population on the basis of a sample. Instead, its objective is to uncover at least one instance of a suspected serious problem, such as fraud or a substantial mistake or compliance failure.

This sampling approach is most appropriate to use:
- When the expected deviation rate (deviation from expected controls, policies, or laws) is low and the internal auditor wants to design a sample based on a specified probability of finding one occurrence.
- When management policy is for zero tolerance of noncompliance or error in a given area. The audit decision is made once the first error is observed.

One of the major challenges of using discovery sampling to confirm or allay suspicions of a serious problem is to determine a sample size that is:
- Accurately predictive.
- Reasonable. (Statistical sampling allows the internal auditor to demonstrate "reasonableness"—to be sure that the sample is large enough to include at least one example of a suspected serious problem or fraud but small enough to merit the cost of investigation.)

Two commonly used methods of discovery sampling are:

- Random sampling.
- Dollar-unit discovery sampling.

In both cases, the size of the sample is influenced by statistical theory and the cost and/ or goals of the audit. Organizational goals may vary. Some organizations may calculate that they will tolerate a given percentage or dollar amount of fraud; the sample size selected for the audit will reflect this accepted risk level. Internal auditors may use statistical tables to define their sample sizes once the organization has defined its tolerance for risk.

Nonstatistical Sampling

Nonstatistical sampling must project the sample results to the population as it is unable to quantify sampling risk statistically. Auditors must determine whether they can reach valid conclusions using nonstatistical sampling as opposed to more costly and time-consuming statistical sampling approaches.

Nonstatistical sampling allows more latitude regarding sample selection and evaluation, though it must still be a sample thought to be representative of the population.

Nonstatistical Sampling Techniques

Variations of nonstatistical sampling include haphazard sampling and interval sampling.

Haphazard Sampling

Its name indicates that this type of sampling lacks credibility. Instead of using either judgment or random sampling to select a sample, the auditor simply takes whatever items are convenient, without concern for their representative possibilities.

This is not random sampling, although in common language it would be described as selecting items "at random." The items selected haphazardly may, in fact, not be random at all but may represent some bias on the part of the auditor or may include a number of unrepresentative items that skew the results.

Haphazard sampling occurs, in effect, when a surveyor sends questionnaires to a selected group, such as readers of a particular magazine, and uses responses from those questionnaires returned voluntarily to characterize the entire group of magazine subscribers (or, worse yet, all readers, or even worse, the larger community). Since the selected sample contains only those interested enough to respond, it is in no sense random and is very likely biased toward some shared characteristic of the respondents.

Interval Sampling

Instead of using random numbers, an auditor may decide to choose items that are a certain interval apart on a list. For instance, to select a sample of 50 items from a population of 1,000, the auditor might select every 20th item starting at a randomly selected point—numbers 10, 30, 50, 70, etc. (The starting point should be less than 20.)

This method of sampling may fail to generate random items if the list contains some sort of bias. For some reason, the list may be clustered in groups of 20 and every 20th item may have the same characteristic (one supervisor followed by 19 employees, for example). To control for that possibility, the auditor might take three samples of items 60 numbers apart, starting from three randomly selected points in the list (below 60).

Sampling Risk

Sampling risk is the risk that the internal auditor's conclusion based on sample testing may be different than the conclusion reached if the audit procedure were applied to all items in the population. There are specific risks associated with assessing control risk too high and assessing it too low.

- When assessing control risk too low, the auditor incorrectly concludes that a specified control is more effective than it really is. This is sometimes called the risk of over-reliance.
- Assessing control risk too high occurs when the internal auditor will incorrectly conclude that a specified control is less effective than it really is. This is sometimes called the risk of under-reliance.

Chapter 2: Analysis and Evaluation

Data analysis and evaluation involve comparing information gathered during an engagement to the expectations regarding that information. Internal auditors develop expectations about what is typical or expected of a process or function during audit planning. This provides a basis against which reasonableness can be determined. Expectations are based in part on evidence from prior audits or other sources and in part on forward-looking considerations, such as organizational objectives, the objectives of the process or function, significant risks, and the organization's risk appetite.

When data does not conform to what should be reasonably expected, such as an anomaly, a variance, or an unexpected correlation, the auditor interprets this difference as evidence that there is an unaccounted-for condition or force acting on the relationship in question. The auditor should form his or her own conclusions as to the causes of these differences and whether they are likely to be isolated events or trends. It is important to perform this independent interpretation prior to seeking out the interpretations of the audit client and other sources such as industry or economic trends, as this can help guard against inheriting a bias from such sources. If such sources provide corroboration, it becomes more evidence of the reliability of the interpretation. If other explanations disagree, then further analysis and interpretation may be needed.

With audit software and the advancement of technology, auditors may be analyzing "big data" and can often test 100% of transactions using newer systems and tools. Artificial intelligence advances may also help make audit tests more efficient and effective.

The topics in this chapter address computerized audit tools and techniques, sources of evidence, process mapping and analytical review techniques, workpapers and documentation, and engagement conclusions.

Topic A: Computerized Audit Tools and Techniques

This topic discusses how auditors can make use of ever-improving technology to perform audits with greater efficiency and accuracy.

CAATs

Common computer-assisted auditing techniques (CAATs) include:
- Automated workpapers.
- Utility software.
- Test data.
- Application software tracing and mapping.
- Audit expert systems.
- Continuous auditing.
- Generalized audit software (GAS).

Internal auditors can use CAATs to directly test controls built into computerized information systems and data contained in computer files. By testing data contained in computer files, internal auditors obtain indirect evidence about the effectiveness of the controls in the application that processed the data.

CAATs are automated techniques enabling auditors to test large populations of data efficiently. Data analysis using CAATs creates the option of continuous auditing, allowing ongoing testing of 100% of transactions. Continuous monitoring is a method of testing controls more frequently. Use of continuous monitoring and auditing can significantly reduce instances of error, risk, and fraud.

Topic B: Evaluating Potential Sources of Evidence

This topic discusses how auditors should approach the requirement that they use sufficient, relevant, reliable, and trustworthy sources of information when conducting an engagement.

In addition to reviewing the contents of this topic, students can review the following IIA materials:
- Implementation Guidance for Standard 2310

Relevance, Sufficiency, and Reliability

Performance Standard 2310, "Identifying Information"

Internal auditors must identify sufficient, reliable, relevant, and useful information to achieve the engagement's objectives.

The information characteristics listed in Standard 2310 can be described as follows:
- Sufficient information is factual, adequate, and convincing so that a prudent, informed person would reach the same conclusions as the auditor.
- Reliable information is the best attainable information through the use of appropriate engagement techniques.
- Relevant information supports engagement observations and recommendations and is consistent with the objectives for the engagement.
- Useful information helps the organization meet its goals.

These characteristics are covered in greater detail elsewhere.

Auditors begin gathering information, which includes audit evidence, when planning the engagements. Helpful actions when planning the engagement include reviewing:
- The engagement objectives and engagement work program.
- Organizational policies.
- Jurisdictional laws. (It may also be helpful to consult with the organization's legal counsel.)

The process of gathering information is facilitated by open and collaborative communication between the internal auditor and the organization's personnel, which is accomplished by:
- Maintaining effective channels of communication.
- Organizational independence (Standard 1110).

The level of analysis and detail applied during the planning phase varies by internal audit activity and engagement. The reliability of audit information depends on the use of appropriate engagement techniques.

Simple manual audit procedures include:

- Inspecting physical evidence.
- Examining documentation from the audit client or outside sources.
- Gathering testimonial evidence.
- Conducting a walkthrough to observe a process in action.
- Examining continuously monitored data.

Due to resource constraints, internal auditors should identify and prioritize the most relevant and useful information and critically assess all engagement information as a whole.

Conformance with Standard 2310 may be demonstrated in the engagement work program and supporting engagement workpapers. To confirm the usefulness of information provided, surveys could be issued after engagement communications are completed.

Evidence Considerations

The internal auditor also needs to consider matters of source, availability, confidentiality, and access as they relate to audit evidence.

- **Source**. The source of the audit evidence can add to, or detract from, its persuasiveness. **Corroborative evidence** directly obtained from an independent third party can be more reliable than audit evidence from the organization being audited. Third-party evidence may be called external evidence to distinguish it from internal evidence provided by the audit customer.

  The strength or weakness of the evidence depends on how persuasive it is. A source is persuasive if it enables the internal auditor to formulate well-founded conclusions and advice confidently. To be persuasive, the source of evidence must be sufficient, reliable, relevant, and useful.

- **Availability**. The internal auditor should consider the time during which evidence will be available for testing. This applies especially when the evidence is stored electronically. Audit evidence processed by electronic data interchange (EDI), document image processing (DIP), and dynamic systems such as spreadsheets may not be retrievable after a specified period of time if files are revised without being controlled or backed up. Security and other recordings may be on a loop system, where data is over-written with new information if not gathered in a timely fashion.

- **Confidentiality**. The internal auditor should always bear in mind the mandatory injunction, in The IIA's Code of Ethics, to honor the confidentiality requirements of the owners of audited data. This may become even more challenging as audit data increasingly resides on servers connected throughout an organization and, quite likely, to the rest of the wired world.

When extracting data from computer databases by means of computer-assisted audit techniques, the auditor needs to exercise special care not to distribute sensitive information to unauthorized sources or to corrupt data in the process of extraction.

- **Access**. The internal audit activity must have free access to the evidence that it requires when conducting an engagement, as noted in Standard 1110.A1.

Implementation Standard 1110.A1 (Assurance Engagements)

The internal audit activity must be free from interference in determining the scope of internal auditing, performing work, and communicating results. The chief audit executive must disclose such interference to the board and discuss the implications.

Evaluating Sources of Evidence

Audit evidence should be the best available to the auditor in terms of its sufficiency, reliability, relevance, and usefulness.

- **Sufficiency**. Sufficient means that there should be enough evidence and that different but related pieces of evidence should corroborate each other. Sufficiency is therefore assessed for the body of evidence as a whole. The sufficiency of evidence will necessarily be subject to interpretation by different observers, depending on factors such as the extent of their relevant knowledge and, perhaps, their biases. Sometimes evidence must not only be sufficient but must be presented in such a way that its sufficiency is obvious to the audience.

In order to promote sufficiency of evidence throughout the internal audit activity, the CAE should establish a system of documentation, including preferred terminology and standardized notations, to be used consistently.

- **Reliability**. Reliability implies that the evidence must come from a credible source. This considers whether or not the internal auditor directly obtained the evidence. The reliability (or competence) of audit information also depends upon the type of evidence. Sampling techniques may be disputed as to their reliability as a basis for conclusions about the larger population. Audit conclusions should be supported by the most reliable evidence that is available to the auditor.

Due to the prevalence of photograph editing software, photographs are considered to be hearsay and should be corroborated by competent testimony.

- **Relevance**. Evidence may be reliable in itself, but it is of no use if it is not relevant to the matter at hand. Relying on evidence that has little or no pertinence increases audit risk—the risk of reaching invalid conclusions and providing faulty advice.

- **Usefulness**. The usefulness of information is a function of whether the information is germane to the organization. The information's timeliness can make a difference in whether it is useful or not (i.e., ability of the information to influence decisions currently being made).

Topic C: Analytical Approaches and Process Mapping

This topic discusses some of the analytical approaches and process mapping techniques that auditors may use when examining and analyzing information gathered during an engagement.

In addition to reviewing the contents of this topic, students can review the following IIA materials:
- Implementation Guidance for Standard 2320

Analytics and Process Mapping

Performance Standard 2320, "Analysis and Evaluation"

Internal auditors must base conclusions and engagement results on appropriate analysis and evaluations.

Performing the engagement involves conducting the tests prescribed in the work program. Based on the risk and control matrix and work program, internal auditors are likely to have a specific list of procedures and tests to be conducted. Other factors established in the work program include:

- Management assertions.
- Testing:
  - Objectives.
  - Criteria.
  - Approach.
  - Procedures.
  - Population.
- Sampling methodology.
- Sample sizes.

Ultimately, auditors seek to reach conclusions as a result of executing the work program. Conclusions on whether existing controls are adequate to help achieve the objectives of the area or process requires sufficient information about:

- Design adequacy.
- Operating effectiveness of controls.

The testing extent depends on whether test results have produced sufficient audit evidence on which to base conclusions or advice.

- If proscribed testing doesn't provide sufficient information, adjustments to the testing plan and additional testing may be required.
- Note that Standard 2240.A1 requires adjustments to the work program to be approved promptly.

Testing approaches combine manual audit procedures and computer-assisted audit techniques (CAATs). Testing may look at a complete population or a representative sample of information. If using a sample, methods must be used to ensure that the whole population and/or time period are adequately represented by the sample.

Simple manual procedures include gathering information through inquiry, observation, and inspection. Other procedures include:

- **Vouching**. Internal auditors test the validity of documented or recorded information by following it backward to a tangible resource or a previously prepared record.

- **Tracing**. Internal auditors test the completeness of documented or recorded information by tracking information forward from a document, record, or tangible resource to a subsequently prepared document.

- **Reperformance**. Internal auditors test the accuracy of a control by reperforming the task, which may provide direct evidence of the control's operating effectiveness.

- **Independent confirmation**. Internal auditors solicit and obtain written verification of the accuracy of information from an independent third party.

Processes that are examined during the engagement may be documented in a process map. Some of the most common forms include:

- Flowcharts.
- Narratives.
- Block diagrams.
- Spaghetti maps.
- RACI diagrams.

These are discussed below.

Flowcharts

Next to personal inspection, process documentation is most commonly achieved through the use of flowcharts. A **flowchart** is a graphical representation of the actual or ideal path followed by any service or product. It provides a visual sequence of the steps in a process, illustrates the relationships between parts, and identifies what the process does or should do. Flowcharts range from simple to complex, depending on the level of detail shown. They are effective because they are easy to understand and therefore practical to review with the audit client. A flowchart eliminates abstractions about how work flows through a system.

Flowcharts can be created in a variety of ways, such as:
- Highly informal pencil drawings on paper.
- Technically sophisticated computer graphics.
- Mapping the sequence using Post-it™ notes, arranging and rearranging a sequence until stakeholders reach agreement.

Common symbols used in flowcharts are shown in Exhibit 2-12.

Exhibit 2-12: Standard Flowchart Symbols

☐	Process	☐	Document
◇	Decision point	☐	Document (multipage)
▱	Input/output	⬭	Start or end of process
⬭	Online storage	◯	On-page connector (for example, to refer to instructions elsewhere on the page)
⬭	Database		
▽	Manual file (may also be used to mean "merge"; flipped over—with the base down—it can mean "extract")	⬡	Off-page connector (for example, to refer to a related flowchart on a another page)

The auditor can develop a flowchart of any process, from the process of the audit itself to the processes to be audited. When each proposed or existing step has been placed on the map, the auditor and other reviewers can more readily assess:
- Which steps are crucial.
- Which steps can be omitted.
- Where steps should be sequenced differently.
- Where new steps should be added.

In the process of creating the flowchart, participants may discover points of weakness in controls, or they may discover that what they believe to be an accurate representation of a process is not actually what is observed by the internal auditor.

During the planning phase of an engagement, internal auditors may review existing flowcharts or they may prepare new flowcharts. When reviewing an existing flowchart, an internal auditor:

- Can make a preliminary assessment about the identification of risks or the adequacy of controls.
- Can make a preliminary assessment about whether there are unnecessary controls in the process.
- Should verify that the flowchart is current and accurately reflects the process.

Flowchart Formats

Flowcharts can be laid out either vertically or horizontally. While merely practical considerations of space may determine the better format, more significant considerations may influence this choice. For example, one format may favor the flow of a process through particular units (or functions) of the organization, while another may emphasize the process flow with less reference to organizational units—or none at all.

In Exhibit 2-13, you can see the same process laid out in three different ways. The process charted includes the scheduling, pressing, assembly, and inspection of components. Note that the inspections function appears at two different points in the process, complicating the map.

- The horizontal chart emphasizes the horizontal flow of the steps in the overall process, moving from left to right. It includes a reference to the functions involved in the process (scheduling, pressing, assembly, and inspection), but they are de-emphasized and moved to the far left side of the diagram.

- The vertical flowchart emphasizing flow through departments uses a combination of horizontal and vertical structures, placing the function names in a more prominent position at the top.

- The third process map places all the process steps in a vertical flow and eliminates any reference to the functions. The process itself is most easily followed in this format, but it does eliminate relevant information about functions.

Exhibit 2-13: Cross-Functional Flowcharts

Horizontal format emphasizing the steps in the process

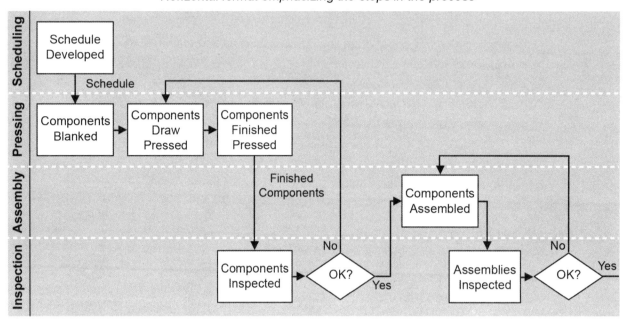

Vertical format emphasizing flow through departments

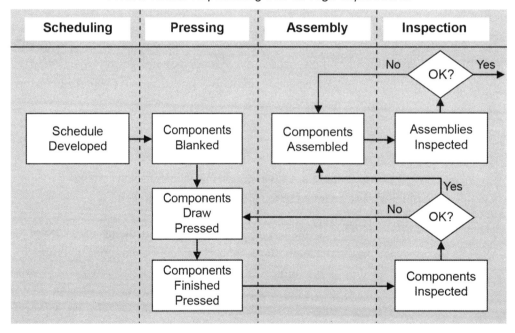

Vertical format emphasizing process flow

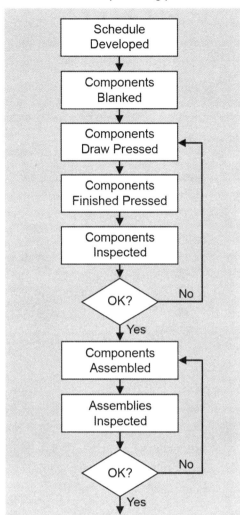

The internal auditor should use the type of flowchart that best suits the process being defined. Care should be taken to accurately document the actual process and avoid unnecessary complexity.

Flowcharts can yield much useful information for internal auditors as well as the client by providing:

- A clear picture of how a process works by illustrating the relationship of various steps and control points.
- A common reference point and standard language for talking about an existing process or project during an audit engagement.

Narratives

Narratives provide a step-by-step picture of a process in a single document without the use of detailed symbols or keys. Similar to a flowchart, the purpose of a narrative is to identify the key controls and cases of under- or over-control and processing redundancy.

Narratives are the documentation methodology many organizations use to describe simple processes and activities performed to achieve process objectives. They can provide more detailed information about the steps in a process than flowcharts, and they are therefore often used to augment a flowchart and provide context and nuance. Narratives are flexible and facilitate open-ended questioning. However, there is no inherent discipline or standardization in how to prepare a narrative; several renditions are possible. For some organizations, narratives work well and provide meaningful information. For others, the format may not be complete enough and the lack of standardization may increase the likelihood of missing key issues or control weaknesses and may be difficult for an internal auditor to follow.

Block Diagrams

A **block diagram** is a pictorial representation of a process or activity, typically including a series of boxes and connecting lines to indicate association and direction/ order. Quick and simple to construct, they can be used to show the flow of information and organizational arrangements. Block diagrams are sometimes used in lieu of flowcharts because of their simplicity. Exhibit 2-14 is an example of a block diagram showing the evaluation of job descriptions.

Exhibit 2-14: Sample Block Diagram for Evaluating Job Descriptions

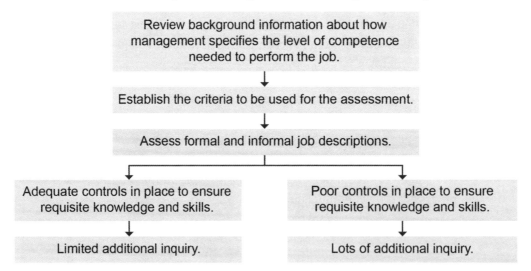

Block diagrams are useful for high-level representations and are not appropriate for detailed analysis.

Spaghetti Maps

Spaghetti maps are Six Sigma diagrams limited in scope to a particular area. They are used to track the flow of:

- Products.
- People.
- Paperwork.

Multiple flows can be documented using different line colors. One might visually map, on graph paper, the actual steps an operator takes in one instance of a normal operation (not the idealized process or unusual situations).

The process is conducted in a series of steps:

1. The various stations are placed on the diagram using simple boxes. The distance between stations represents the actual distances, for example, one box on the graph paper could represent an actual square foot or square meter.

2. The operator's path is added to the diagram, starting at the first step. If the operator goes between places more than once, lines are added, even if they overlap. This can reveal instances when exceptions to an idealized flow are actually fairly common.

3. The time the process is taking is also recorded, including delays such as waiting for materials or tools.

4. The lines on the map are then used to calculate the actual distance traveled.

5. The internal auditor and area specialists discuss how the process could be improved to reduce distance and time.

6. Improvements are documented in text and in a new diagram.

Exhibit 2-15 shows a "before" version of a spaghetti map for screen door manufacturing; Exhibit 2-16 shows the "after" version.

Exhibit 2-15: Spaghetti Map, "Before" Version

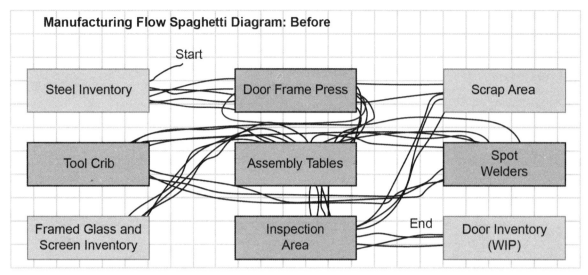

Distance: Screen door assembler traveled 2,650 ft. to assemble first good unit.
Setup time: 72 minutes from last good unit of prior run to first good piece of new run.

Exhibit 2-16: Spaghetti Map, "After" Version

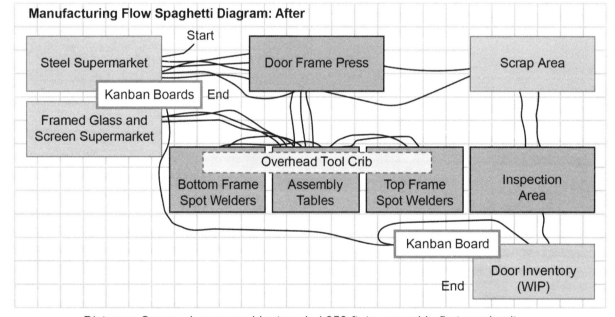

Distance: Screen door assembler traveled 850 ft. to assemble first good unit.
Setup time: 26 minutes from last good unit of prior run to first good piece of new run.

RACI Charts

RACI stands for:

- **Responsible**. This means that the person will perform the activity or process, perhaps alongside others listed in the chart.

- **Accountable**. This means that the person will be answerable for the success or failure of the activity or deliverable in question. This may be a supervisor, for example.

- **Consulted**. This means that the stakeholder should be communicated with regarding the process or area and that he or she has a say in various decisions that need to be made. This could be an expert or a senior manager.

- **Informed**. This means that the stakeholder needs to be kept up to date on the situation or relevant matters but does not have a say in decisions being made

A RACI chart lists the various stakeholders of a process or area in rows and columns for R, A, C, and I. An X or check mark is placed in the chart to indicate whether a party has one or more of these designations.

A simple example of a RACI chart is shown in Exhibit 2-17.

Exhibit 2-17: RACI Chart

IT hiring process	HR specialist	IT manager	IT director
Screen candidates	R	I	I
Interview candidates	C	R	I
Select candidate	I	R	A/C
Extend offer	R	I	I
Onboarding	R	A	I

R = Responsible for task completion   A = Accountable for outcome
C = Consulted (provides input on the work)   I = Informed of progress

Topic D: Analytical Review Techniques

This topic discusses how analytical procedures are used to compare information against expectations and how auditors can evaluate that information during the engagement.

In addition to reviewing the contents of this topic, students can review the following IIA materials:
- Implementation Guidance for Standard 2320
- Implementation Guidance for Standard 2330

Analytical Review Techniques

An **analytical review** (also referred to as **analytical auditing** or analytical procedures) examines relationships among information. In particular, examining relationships among information that is often overlooked can provide valuable insights.

The information examined may be:
- Financial.
- Nonfinancial.
- Quantitative.
- Qualitative.

Typical measures internal auditors use during an analytical review include:
- Monetary amounts.
- Inventory quantities.
- Ratios.
- Percentages.

Analytical reviews are used during different phases of the audit engagement:

- During a preliminary survey, analytical reviews are used at a high level to substantiate the internal auditor's engagement plan. This helps:
  - Ensure that the audit scope is appropriate.
  - Identify conditions for further investigation during fieldwork.

- During fieldwork, they are used to:
  - Evaluate the data or samples collected.
  - Develop findings, conclusions, and recommendations.

Information is evaluated based on the experience, logic, and professional skepticism of the internal auditor. According to Standard 2330, auditors must document information that logically supports the engagement results and conclusions.

Root cause analysis is often used to identify the underlying reason for the occurrence of an error, a problem, a missed opportunity, or an instance of noncompliance. This enables internal auditors to add insights but sometimes requires extensive resources. Thus, undertaking such analysis must be done only after considering the effort in relation to the potential benefits, in accordance with Standard 1220.A1.

Selecting Analytical Procedures

When selecting an analytical procedure, internal auditors should consider:

- The significance of the area being examined.
- The assessment of risk and the effectiveness of risk management in the area being examined.
- The availability and reliability of financial and nonfinancial information.
- The precision with which the results of analytical procedures can be predicted.
- The availability and comparability of information regarding the industry in which the organization operates.
- The extent to which other engagement procedures provide support for engagement results.

Internal auditors should add an analytical procedure only when it helps to prove a point relevant to the engagement objective. This requires internal auditors to determine what the procedure can and cannot prove and compare this to the engagement objective.

Analytical Techniques

Whatever the type of measurement employed, the purpose of analytical comparisons is always to assist the auditor in identifying conditions that may warrant further inquiry. Specific analytic techniques include (but are not limited to) those shown below.

• Reasonableness tests	• Regression analysis
• Variance analysis	• Cause-and-effect diagrams
• Trend analysis	• Pareto analysis
• Ratio analysis	

Reasonableness Tests

A key tenet in analytical reviews is the concept of reasonableness, the wise application of the internal auditor's auditing experience and knowledge of the organization and industry to any audit test result. Reasonableness is as much a criterion underlying the other tests described in this topic as it is a specific type of test.

When comparing one set of data to another, the auditor expects to find reasonable relationships among pieces of information. If unexpected differences are found when comparing information or, conversely, expected differences are absent, the internal auditor needs to make a judgment as to whether the change or consistency is reasonable. If the answer is no, the internal audit activity should investigate the reason for this during the engagement.

Variance Analysis

Variance analysis is a fundamental type of analytical procedure that begins with the recognition that one set of data differs from another set in an unexpected way. Variance analysis can also be used for:

- Comparison of the objectives for the activity or process being audited to organizational objectives.
- Analysis of the factors that have caused a difference between a planned or standard amount and the actual results.
- Comparison of the timeliness of how actual products and services are delivered against area and organizational objectives.
- Comparison of financial data for a current period with similar data of one or more past periods.
- IT analysis practices to compare data discrepancies between two databases (such as names or addresses between human resources and payroll files).

Budgets are a common focus of variance analysis. Although budgets can be scrutinized from many different perspectives (credibility, amount of slack, efficiency, effectiveness, growth or diminishment, etc.), in each instance variance analysis can be used to compare one set of budgetary numbers with another set that provides a standard for evaluation.

For example, the projected month-by-month budget might be compared with actual expenditures for each month to uncover any unreasonable discrepancies. The current period expense budget might be compared to the same expenses for a previous period or to an industry average.

Exhibit 2-18 illustrates a simple variance analysis for an annual budget when compared against actual expenses, first in table form and then as a chart.

Exhibit 2-18: Analysis of Variance Between Actual and Budgeted Amounts

Period	Projected Marketing Expense (USD)	Actual Marketing Expense (USD)
January	$9,000	$8,500
February	10,000	8,500
March	10,500	8,500
April	10,500	9,500
May	10,500	10,500
June	10,000	12,000
July	10,000	16,000

 v7.0

Period	Projected Marketing Expense (USD)	Actual Marketing Expense (USD)
August	12,500	13,000
September	13,000	11,000
October	12,500	9,000
November	9,500	8,000
December	9,000	12,500
Total	127,000	127,000

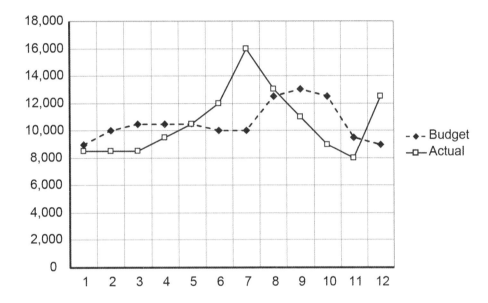

Trend Analysis

Trend analysis, also known as horizontal analysis, is the most common analytical audit technique. It traces relationships in historical financial or operational data as they evolve over time. Trend analysis is often used to:

- Identify performance indicators.
- Highlight significant changes.
- Evaluate the present position.

It may be categorized as long- or short-range.

- Long-range trend analysis examines performance data over an extended period of time with the intent of prioritizing improvement actions on the basis of the performance trends.
- Short-range trend analysis identifies areas of potential process or system improvements.

Trends subject to analysis are many and varied. Some examples of trends commonly analyzed are:

• Revenues.
• Expenses.
• Store openings.
• Production.
• Profits.

Trends can also be traced for ratios, either financial ratios, such as the trend in the price/earnings ratio for common stock, or operating ratios, such as production cycles or units of product per hours of labor.

Trend analysis is often used to review the changes in an account balance or another series of historical data. Because of its focus on historical sequences of data, it is more appropriately used in reviewing data from income statements or expense accounts than from balance sheets, which present financial information for a particular point in time.

Although its use is associated with scrutiny of financial accounts, trend analysis can also be applied to operating information. It can be used in the comparison of similar data from repetitive audits and in the comparison of organizational activities to industry activities.

A specialized form of trend analysis is known as the learning curve, which tracks the trend in productivity in relation to the increased efficiency of workers as they become familiar with equipment, procedures, etc. Exhibit 2-19 illustrates the general shape of a learning curve, which is, in effect, a trend analysis of the impact of experience upon efficiency.

Exhibit 2-19: Learning Curve

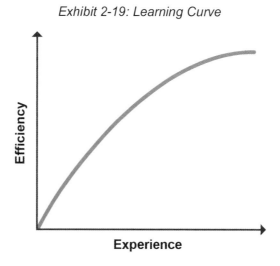

The trend tracked by the learning curve generally moves upward relatively rapidly at first as workers gain experience with the job in question and do it more effectively. Eventually the impact of more experience becomes negligible, and the curve levels off.

As is the case with learning curves, the purpose of trend analysis is to evaluate the impact of one variable, such as experience, upon another variable, such as efficiency or effectiveness.

The shape of the curve can tell an auditor whether the relationship between the variables is trending in the right or wrong direction. If the curve in the exhibit were charting the relationship between, say, output on the vertical axis and investment on the horizontal axis, you might conclude that any further increases in investment would be wasted, since additional dollars were no longer resulting in higher output.

Trend analysis might be used to track the impact of additional workers on production output. A graph of that situation might show that added workers increase output up to a point, after which output flattens as the added workers outstrip the capacity of available equipment and become redundant.

Ratio Analysis

Ratios are mathematical relationships among two or more numbers, often stated in the form of percentages, times, or days. They compare relationships at a specific point in time. Ratio analysis generally computes and interprets these ratios; it can be employed in comparison of relationships between similar divisions in the organization, perhaps in different countries. Examples of commonly used ratios are provided in Part 3 of this learning system.

Regression Analysis

Regression analysis is a statistical technique used to measure the amount of change in one value in relation to a change in another value. In simpler applications of the method, regression equations show the impact that one variable has on one other. The method is not limited to financial variables or to variables of the same type. Regression analysis can be used to examine the impact of a nonfinancial variable on a financial variable (or vice versa), such as the impact of increasing the size of a sales force on sales revenues. One of the benefits of regression analysis is its adaptability to track relationships among many different kinds of variables.

The regression equation can be used by management to project future budgets based on experience with past budgets or on other measures, and it can be used by an auditor to judge the reasonableness of either the budget or the actual results.

In addition to simple regression analyses that involve one independent variable and one dependent variable presumed to be influenced by the independent variable, it is also possible to perform **multiple regression analysis**. This statistical technique is used to trace the effects of more than one independent variable on one dependent variable.

Like any other statistical correlation technique, regression analysis demonstrates, at best, only that one variable changes at the same time as one or more other variables change. It doesn't indicate the reasons for the change. Nor does regression analysis guarantee that the independent variable is in fact the reason for the change observed in the dependent variable.

Cause-and-Effect Diagrams

A **cause-and-effect diagram** (also called a fishbone or Ishikawa diagram) uses a visual to map out a list of factors that are thought to affect a problem or a desired outcome. An audit team might use such a diagram to determine the root cause of a process with many problem elements. An example of a cause-and-effect diagram is shown in Exhibit 2-20.

Exhibit 2-20: Cause-and-Effect Diagram

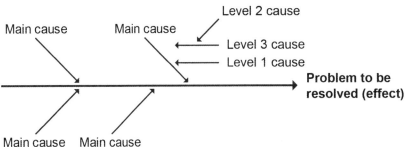

Pareto Analysis

A **Pareto analysis** is based on the 80/20 rule, an observation that 80% of the problems, outputs, or rewards of a process tend to be caused by just 20% of the total causes, inputs, or effort. Internal auditors can use a Pareto analysis to prioritize recommendations on just those key activities, controls, or other changes that are likely to create the greatest effect. For example, Exhibit 2-21 shows the results of internal auditor analysis of controls designed to minimize a department's expenditures.

Exhibit 2-21: Pareto Analysis of Department Expenditure Controls

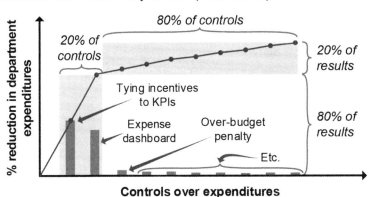

Of these, two key controls appear to have the greatest effect, tying the manager's incentives to key performance indicators for the function and the manager's use of an automated expense dashboard for daily decision making. Other secondary controls contribute to a lesser extent.

Pareto charts can help explain in a visual way the importance of prioritization—such as identifying key controls and making them the audit focus—and can also help convince decision makers to accept recommendations—perhaps to eliminate an ineffective but expensive control.

Topic E: Prepare Workpapers and Documentation

This topic discusses the importance of documentation when building conclusions during the audit engagement and how workpapers are designed to support the documentation process.

In addition to reviewing the contents of this topic, students can review the following IIA materials:
- Implementation Guidance for Standard 2330

Workpapers and Documentation

Performance Standard 2330, "Documenting Information"
Internal auditors must document sufficient, reliable, relevant, and useful information to support the engagement results and conclusions.

Engagement workpapers are used to document the information generated throughout the engagement process, including:
- Planning.
- Testing, analyzing, and evaluating data.
- Formulating engagement results and conclusions.

Workpapers may be maintained electronically, on paper, or in both formats. Consistency, to the extent possible, is important within the internal audit activity to facilitate sharing of information and coordination between audit activities. The CAE is typically responsible for developing guidelines and procedures. Commonly standardized elements include:
- General layout.
- "Tick-mark" notation.
- System for cross-referencing other workpapers.
- Designated information for permanent retention or use in other engagements.

Similar to Standard 2310, the sufficiency, reliability, relevance, and usefulness of the information are key considerations when documenting information in workpapers.

Workpaper documentation is an important part of a systematic and disciplined engagement process because it organizes audit evidence in a way that enables reperformance of the work and supports engagement conclusions and results. Workpapers may include the following elements:

- Index or reference number
- Title or heading that identifies the area or process under review
- Date or period of the engagement
- Scope of the work performed
- Statement of purpose for obtaining and analyzing the data
- Sources of data covered in the workpaper
- Description of population evaluated, including sample size and method of selection
- Methodology used to analyze data
- Details of tests conducted and analyses performed
- Conclusions, including cross-referencing to the workpaper on audit observations
- Proposed follow-up engagement work to be performed
- Name of the internal auditor(s) who performed the engagement work
- Review notation and name of the internal auditor(s) who reviewed the work

Workpapers are generally organized according to the structure developed in the work program and cross-referenced to relevant pieces of information, resulting in a complete collection of documentation of:

- Procedures completed.
- Information obtained.
- Conclusions reached.
- Recommendations derived.
- The logical basis for each of the steps.

This is the primary source of support for the internal auditors' communication with stakeholders, including senior management, the board, and management of the area or process under review.

Supervisory review of workpapers is typically used to develop internal audit staff. This can be accomplished by determining that engagement workpapers adequately support the engagement observations, conclusions, and recommendations. The CAE is responsible for all significant supervisory judgments made during the engagement, including review of workpapers.

Conformance can be demonstrated through properly prepared and completed workpapers. Feedback from stakeholders about the quality of evidence may also be used as well as demonstration of management's effective implementation of recommended actions.

Preparing Workpapers

The content, organization, and format of workpapers generally vary by organization and the nature of the engagement. However, it is important to achieve workpaper consistency within the internal audit activity as much as possible, as it generally helps facilitate sharing of engagement information and coordination of audit activities.

The use of standardized, yet flexible, workpaper formats or templates improves the efficiency and consistency of the engagement process.

Most organizations develop unique workpaper requirements for assurance and consulting engagements. The requirements of the *Standards* and the best practices of the Implementation Guides are used as guidance in the development of the workpaper procedures for the organization.

It is important to note that consulting engagement assignments vary widely in scope and objectives and differ in some fundamental respects from assurance engagements. For example, the consulting client determines the need for the consulting engagement rather than the internal audit activity and, like any client, has considerable influence on the nature and scope of the work. Documenting such engagements in workpapers, therefore, may answer to somewhat different demands than are placed upon assurance workpapers. Nevertheless, the internal auditor acting as consultant is still fully responsible to The IIA's Code of Ethics and *Standards*. And consulting engagements, too, must be documented in workpapers.

Necessary Workpaper Contents

Workpapers should contain the work done during the engagement. This includes virtually everything committed to paper or entered into a computer, from initial plans through the final report—graphics and photos included—and other physical or electronic documents. The test of the sufficiency of the workpapers is that they should document the audit's objectives and methods so thoroughly that a new auditor added to the project at any point could fully comprehend the engagement from the workpapers and bring the audit to a successful conclusion.

Workpaper Policies

Because the CAE is responsible for coordination and for developing the internal audit activity's policies and procedures, it is logical for the CAE to develop guidelines and procedures for completing workpapers for various types of engagements. Standardized engagement working papers, such as questionnaires and audit programs, may improve the engagement's efficiency and facilitate the delegation of engagement work. Engagement working papers may be categorized as permanent or carry-forward engagement files that contain information of continuing importance.

Standards of Style and Order

Workpapers should adhere to high standards of clarity and order. Specifically, they should be:

- **Understandable**. Workpapers should need no supplements to be understandable in terms of what the auditor intended to do, accomplished, discovered, concluded, and decided not to do. Workpapers should balance the need to be concise with the need to be clear.

- **Relevant**. Workpapers should contain only that content that is relevant and material to the engagement objectives. Material that is peripheral should be omitted.

- **Uniform**. Electronic and hard-copy workpapers should be the same format or size. (Small printed workpapers should be attached to standard-size sheets, etc.) Binders help maintain printed workpapers in good order, allow easy modification, and prevent loss.

- **Economical**. Keeping workpapers relevant can also help with economy. Workpapers should not attempt to be all-encompassing, especially when an audit indicates satisfactory conditions. Avoid duplication of effort whenever possible, and answer only as many questions as are necessary to establish a fact. Use workpapers from previous audits as much as possible.

- **Complete**. No relevant question should be left unanswered. If a question cannot be answered, the reason for this should be stated. All cross-reference fields must be filled out. A "to do" checklist should be created and included in the workpapers. All questions raised during supervisor reviews should be answered, and the answers should be presented to the supervisor to sign and date. Previous audit findings should be followed up, and the workpapers should include summaries of prior notes and findings with current status.

- **Simply written**. Jargon and technical or arcane language should be avoided. If there is a reason to include words and phrases the audience may not understand, clear explanations should be included. Statements should be kept short.

- **Logically arranged**. The workpapers should be arranged in segments corresponding to the segments of the audit, for easy reference. Keeping the audit process and the workpapers parallel in structure will make the workpapers useful during and after the audit.

Workpaper Format

The following are typical workpaper format considerations:

- Each engagement workpaper should identify the engagement and describe the paper's contents or purpose using descriptive headings.
- Each workpaper should be signed or initialed and dated by the internal auditor performing the work.
- Each workpaper should contain an index or reference number.
- Audit verification symbols ("tick marks") should be explained (and should be kept uniform throughout the audit).
- Sources of data should be clearly identified.
- Supervisory review of the workpapers should also be evidenced.

Some internal audit departments develop departmental style guides and standardized formats that help to streamline audit procedures and facilitate consistent, high-quality work across engagements. Care and common sense should be used so that workpaper formats are not overly rigid and do not inhibit internal audit ingenuity and creativity.

Media

Workpapers are not restricted to paper files and, in fact, may include a variety of media. Electronic files are common because they are easily:

- Stored.
- Retrieved.
- Backed up.
- Distributed through networks.
- Updated throughout the engagement from different locations.

In addition, workpapers may include portable storage devices, emails, photographs, and videos. Electronic files often allow storage of such media as attachments so that the information can be accessed easily.

Software packages available from multiple vendors include templates for workpapers and other audit communications.

Backup copies should be considered for all media, taking into account their vulnerability to deterioration, loss, and obsolescence.

Some of the benefits of automated workpapers include:

- **Cost savings.** The savings from elimination of physical processes and records that consume time and storage space more than make up for the costs related to setting up and using the automated systems.

- **Convenience**. With transmission possible through the web and other networks, there is no need to transport documents by any physical means, even by walking them across the hall. This frees up staff time for more significant work.

- **Efficient communication and easy reference**. Electronic documents can be transmitted simultaneously to multiple readers, or they can be posted on secure websites for discussion during phone or online conferences. Document links can facilitate moving from an assertion to its proof source (or from any point to any other) as easily as clicking a word or an image—without having to riffle through multiple paper pages.

- **Consistency (standardization)**. With templates, quality standards are easier to meet and information is easier to record, find, and store.

- **Ability to incorporate multimedia documentation**. Electronic workpapers can be illustrated by graphs, control charts, diagrams, digital photos, videos, etc. They can incorporate scanned materials as well.

- **Security**. Although no storage medium is completely secure from physical damage, tampering, or theft, electronic files can be backed up to multiple servers in multiple locations or stored in the cloud. Password protection is a must to protect files, however, and files on the web should be "read only" to protect them from malicious or inadvertent revision.

While automated workpapers offer an organization many benefits, getting up and running requires preparation and presents some challenges.

- **Getting trained**. Although workpaper software may be fairly easy to learn, training is required. Organizations need to plan for the necessary training and schedule it at the right time so that staff is ready to use the software when it's available. A vendor may provide training; otherwise, it may be advisable to bring in a training professional.

- **Making a smooth transition**. Software templates may be close to the formats used on paper, in which case the transition can be relatively seamless. On the other hand, if current procedures for paper documents aren't standardized, setting up the automated system will require creating standardized templates. There may also be a need to customize the software to match the needs of the organization. Not all available packages will be right for every organization's needs. It's necessary, therefore, to research available software in light of the organization's existing systems, networks, etc. Making too many modifications to a workpaper package may void the warranty and make the software incompatible with future upgrades.

- **File deterioration and obsolescence**. Although electronic storage reduces the need for huge warehouses to contain documents and provides greater protection from damage due to fire and natural disasters, it also requires special care if long-term retention is a goal. Paper may seem vulnerable to physical damage, but if carefully stored it can last for centuries—not that many audit workpapers demand such lengthy preservation. As the software in which electronic files were created goes through upgrades—or disappears from the market—recovering the files for use may become problematic. Storage of electronic data creates a new set of demands to be solved by the science of data preservation.

Control of Workpapers

Control of workpapers deserves the careful attention of the internal auditor, the CAE, senior management, and, sometimes, legal counsel, because of the following.

- **Workpapers are crucial to the engagement**. Workpapers are crucial to the success of the engagement, since they are the main support for conclusions and recommendations; they may even be critical to the engagement's survival. If workpapers are lost, misplaced, or stolen, the engagement stumbles to a halt and then returns to the starting line. Consequently, the internal auditor should know at all times where the workpapers are and should be equally certain that they are secure. As noted before, workpapers should always be sufficiently up to date and in good order so that a new internal auditor could use them to become familiar with, and complete, the engagement. Electronic workpapers should be "read only" for all users except the auditor, who should be the only person to make changes in the documents.

- **Workpapers may contain confidential or personal information**. The information in workpapers may include personal data about members of the organization, proprietary information, or data with possible legal ramifications. For these reasons, workpapers should be shown only to those authorized to see them.

Implementation Standard 2330.A1 (Assurance Engagements)

The chief audit executive must control access to engagement records. The chief audit executive must obtain the approval of senior management and/or legal counsel prior to releasing such records to external parties, as appropriate.

The CAE must control engagement record access and obtain approval for the release of records to external parties. Requests for access to records by other members of the organization or by external auditors should be subject to approval according to the guidelines in Implementation Guide 2330.

Backup copies of workpapers should remain in the control of the audit department.

Implementation Standard 2330.A2 (Assurance Engagements)

The chief audit executive must develop retention requirements for engagement records, regardless of the medium in which each record is stored. These retention requirements must be consistent with the organization's guidelines and any pertinent regulatory or other requirements.

The CAE should develop policies regarding post-audit retention of workpapers and all engagement records. At the end of an audit engagement, workpaper files should be cleared out so that they contain only the final versions of the documents. Typically, audit departments retain workpapers for a minimum of seven years unless those documents are part of an ongoing investigation. Workpapers should be maintained in a secure location and access restricted.

Implementation Standard 2330.C1 (Consulting Engagements)

The chief audit executive must develop policies governing the custody and retention of consulting engagement records, as well as their release to internal and external parties. These retention requirements must be consistent with the organization's guidelines and any pertinent regulatory or other requirements.

In regard to control and retention of records from consulting engagements, internal auditors are encouraged to adopt appropriate policies and address related issues, such as ownership of consulting engagement records, in order to protect the organization adequately and to avoid potential misunderstandings. Situations that may call for special handling of certain consulting engagement records include those involving:

- Legal proceedings.
- Regulatory requirements.
- Tax issues.
- Accounting matters.

Topic F: Engagement Conclusions

This topic discusses how auditors create engagement conclusions, including what auditors may include in conclusions that are presented to engagement stakeholders.

In addition to reviewing the contents of this topic, students can review the following IIA materials:
- Implementation Guidance for Standard 2410
- Practice Guide, "Audit Reports: Communicating Assurance Engagement Results"
- Practice Guide, "Formulating and Expressing Internal Audit Opinions"

Engagement Conclusions with Risk and Control Assessment

 Performance Standard 2410, "Criteria for Communicating"

Communications must include the engagement's objectives, scope, and results.

When planning the final engagement communication, internal auditors will consider factors including:
- The scope of the engagement.
- Any scope limitations.
- Engagement results.

 Implementation Standard 2410.A2 (Assurance Engagements)

Internal auditors are encouraged to acknowledge satisfactory performance in engagement communications.

Whether and how frequently satisfactory performance should be acknowledged correlates with:
- The expectations of users of the communications.
- How notable the performance is.

Note that communication around consulting engagement conclusions will depend on the nature of the engagement, as described in Standard 2410.C1.

 Implementation Standard 2410.C1 (Consulting Engagements)

Communication of the progress and results of consulting engagements will vary in form and content depending upon the nature of the engagement and the needs of the client.

Final communication includes the internal audit activity's:
- Assessment of the design adequacy and operating effectiveness of the area's controls.
- Rating of the area if a rating system is used.

Control Adequacy and Effectiveness

The internal audit activity provides varying degrees of assurance about the effectiveness of the control processes in place. The activity should have in place an established process for auditing and reporting control issues.

A competent evaluation of the effectiveness of controls entails assessing the controls in the context of risks to objectives. To evaluate the controls, the following should be considered:

- Were significant discrepancies or weaknesses discovered from the audit work performed and other assessment information gathered?
- If so, were corrections or improvements made after the discoveries?
- Do the discoveries and their consequences lead to the conclusion that a pervasive condition exists resulting in an unacceptable level of business risk?

The temporary existence of a significant risk management and control discrepancy or weakness does not necessarily lead to the judgment that it is pervasive and poses an unacceptable residual risk. Factors to be considered in determining whether the effectiveness of the whole system of controls is jeopardized and unacceptable risks exist include:

- The pattern of discoveries.
- The degree of intrusion.
- The level of consequences and exposures.

The report states the critical role played by the control processes in the achievement of the organization's objectives. It also describes the nature and extent of the work performed by the internal audit activity and the nature and extent of reliance on other assurance providers in formulating the opinion.

Results

As dictated by Standard 2410, after the internal auditor has completed all the research for an assurance or consulting engagement, with complete documentation in the workpapers, the time has come to communicate to the audit client in a final report the results of all:

- Testing.
- Sampling.
- Inquiring.
- Recalculating.
- Other research.

Observations

Internal auditors report observations after describing their audit tests and processes but before presenting any findings or conclusions. In this way, facts are kept logically separate from any interpretation that follows.

Findings

Findings organize the facts discovered during audit research. More precisely, they organize the facts the auditor thinks the audit client should know about and, most likely, act upon.

A finding is generally considered to have the following parts, commonly referred to as the five Cs:

- **Criteria**. The criteria are the standards, measures, or expectations used in making an evaluation and/or verification (the correct state).

- **Condition**. The conditions are the objective evidence that the internal auditor finds in the course of the examination (the current state).

- **Cause**. The cause is the reason for the difference between the expected and actual conditions. The identification of the root cause can be a challenge in some engagements. It means identifying what has to be corrected in order to prevent the recurrence of the condition, not just recommending something that would solve the current finding while leaving the underlying cause unresolved.

- **Consequence** (i.e., effect). The consequence is the risk or exposure the organization and/or others encounter because the condition is not consistent with the criteria (the impact of the difference).

- **Corrective action**. The corrective action component of a finding may include recommendations and action plans.

Conclusions

Implementation Standard 2410.A1 (Assurance Engagements)

Final communication of engagement results must include applicable conclusions, as well as applicable recommendations and/or action plans. Where appropriate, the internal auditors' opinion should be provided. An opinion must take into account the expectations of senior management, the board, and other stakeholders and must be supported by sufficient, reliable, relevant, and useful information.

The final engagement communication should include applicable conclusions as well as applicable recommendations and/or action plans.

Conclusions must be documented sufficiently such that someone uninvolved with the original audit can follow along and reach the same conclusion.

A conclusion represents the auditor's professional judgment concerning the activities reviewed in the engagement. Conclusions and opinions are the internal auditor's evaluations of the effects of the observations (the facts) and recommendations on the activities reviewed. They usually put the observations and recommendations in perspective based upon their overall implications.

Conclusions may cover:
- The entire scope of an engagement.
- Specific aspects of an engagement.
- Whether operating objectives and/or goals conform to those of the organization.
- Whether the organization's goals are met.
- Whether the activity under review is functioning as intended.
- Whether internal controls are operating as intended.
- Whether internal controls are efficient.

Any conclusions that appear in the report should be clearly identified.

Opinions

In accordance with Standard 2410.A1, an opinion must take into account the expectations of senior management, the board, and other stakeholders and must be supported by sufficient, reliable, relevant, and useful information. Opinions should communicate crucial information to these stakeholders.

Opinions at the engagement level may be ratings, conclusions, or other descriptions of the results. They may be in relation to controls around a specific process, risk, or business unit. The formulation of such opinions requires consideration of the engagement results and their significance.

Standard 2410.A1 leaves open the option of not rendering an opinion. This should be based on the expectations of the primary stakeholders and may vary based on organization or industry.

When the preference is for inclusion of an opinion, internal auditors should examine not only each finding but also the relationships among the findings.

When opinions are rendered, a best practice is to combine a rating with an opinion description. Ratings structures can vary across organizations and may be split across the following levels:
- Observation
- Opinion
- Report

When the internal audit activity is asked to provide opinions on the overall adequacy of governance, risk management, and control in the organization, the requests may be for an assurance or opinion at a broad level for the organization as a whole (macro-level opinion) or on individual components of the organization's operations (micro-level opinion).

The *Standards* don't require opinions at a macro level. However, without such an opinion, there are potential gray areas for interpretation.

The IPPF glossary differentiates between engagement opinions and overall opinions:

- An **engagement opinion** is a rating, conclusion, and/or other description of results of an individual internal audit engagement, relating to those aspects within the objectives and scope of the engagement.

- An **overall opinion** is a rating, conclusion, and/or other description of results provided by the CAE addressing, at a broad level, governance, risk management, and/or control processes of the organization. An overall opinion is the professional judgment of the CAE based on the results of a number of individual engagements and other activities for a specific time interval.

The communication of an overall opinion will include:
- The scope, including the time period to which the opinion pertains.
- The scope limitations.
- Consideration of all related projects, including the reliance on other assurance providers.
- A summary of the information that supports the opinion.
- The risk or control framework or other criteria used as a basis for the overall opinion.
- The overall opinion, judgment, or conclusion reached.

The reasons for an unfavorable overall opinion must be stated.

If the CAE is asked to provide an opinion, the opinion should clearly specify:
- The evaluation criteria and structure used (such as the COSO internal control framework) and the scope to which the opinion applies.
- That management has responsibility for the establishment and maintenance of internal controls.

In addition, there should be an explanation of the specific type of opinion being expressed by the auditor and what it means regarding the strength of internal controls, as terms may have different meanings in different environments. For example:

- **Positive assurance** (reasonable assurance) is the highest level of assurance and one of the strongest types of audit opinions; therefore, it is most preferred. Different ratings may be used, such as that internal controls are satisfactory or unsatisfactory, effective or ineffective, meet expectations or don't meet expectations, etc. Variations include the use of grading systems.

- **Negative assurance** (limited assurance) indicates that nothing came to the internal auditor's attention that would indicate inadequate internal controls. Such an opinion is less valuable than positive assurance, as it provides limited assurance that sufficient evidence was gathered to determine whether internal controls are inadequate.

- In a **qualified opinion**, specific findings contradict ("qualify") the overall opinion. This type of opinion can be useful in situations where there is an exception to the general opinion. For example, a qualified opinion may indicate that controls were satisfactory, with the exception of accounts payable controls, which require significant improvement.

The CAE should ensure that the opinion expression and scope are consistent with the internal audit activity's board-approved charter and supported by sufficient audit evidence. The CAE should also be aware of the intended audience and potential use for the opinion.

Recommendations

The internal auditor owes management a recommendation for corrective action and should point the way to the continued efficacy of that action.

In formulating recommendations, considerations include:
- The course of action that is most practical and economical in correcting the disparity.
- The objectives that should be kept in mind when recommending corrective action.
- The considerations for management in setting forth an improved course of action.
- The choices and how they measure up when compared with the objectives.
- The best choice with the fewest unsatisfactory side effects.
- The mechanism that should be suggested to control the corrective action after it is taken.

Chapter 3: Engagement Supervision

To ensure that the internal audit function fulfills its charter, meets its key performance indicators, and continually improves the quality of its work, the CAE or designee must maintain oversight of the activity's individual engagements. This chapter describes what is involved in the process of supervision, coordinating work for greater efficiency and effectiveness, and ensuring quality results and continuous improvement.

Topic A: Engagement Supervision Key Activities

This topic covers the key responsibilities that internal audit management has when supervising engagements and the value that proper supervision provides to individual internal auditors.

In addition to reviewing the contents of this topic, students can review the following IIA materials:
- Implementation Guidance for Standard 2340

Supervising Engagements

Performance Standard 2340, "Engagement Supervision"

Engagements must be properly supervised to ensure objectives are achieved, quality is assured, and staff is developed.

The extent of supervision required will depend on the proficiency and experience of internal auditors and the complexity of the engagement. The CAE has the overall responsibility for supervising the engagement but may designate appropriately experienced members of the internal audit activity to perform the review. Appropriate evidence of supervision is to be documented and retained.

The CAE can use previously developed internal audit policies and procedures that address how engagements are planned, performed, and supervised, but determining exactly how the engagement will be supervised will also depend on the specific engagement objectives. The policies and procedures may:
- Specify software programs or templates in order to establish consistent formats.
- Address opportunities for staff development.

Skills assessment of the internal audit staff is an ongoing process, and it generally provides sufficient information about internal auditors' competencies to enable the CAE to appropriately assign internal auditors to engagements based on the auditors':
- Knowledge.
- Skills.
- Other competencies.

Engagement supervision starts during engagement planning and continues throughout the engagement. The engagement supervisor is responsible for approving the work program and may assume responsibility for other aspects of the planning process. The work program must:

- Be designed to achieve the engagement objectives efficiently.
- Include engagement procedures information:
  - Identification
  - Analysis
  - Evaluation
  - Documentation

The engagement supervisor typically maintains ongoing communication with the internal auditor(s) assigned to the engagement and with management of the area or process under review. He or she also:

- Reviews workpapers during the engagement.
- Evaluates whether information, testing, and results are sufficient, reliable, relevant, and useful.
- Reviews engagement communications to ensure that they are:
  - Accurate.
  - Objective.
  - Clear.
  - Concise.
  - Constructive.
  - Complete.
  - Timely.

Throughout the engagement, the supervisor and/or the CAE meet with the internal auditors assigned to the engagement and discuss the engagement process, which provides opportunity for training, development, and evaluation.

Coordinating Work

During initial planning meetings, the auditor-in-charge should communicate specific area assignments and audit tests to audit team members to ensure that:

- All aspects of the work program are covered.
- Work is not duplicated.

The following should also take place:

- Dependent tasks should be clearly identified and acknowledged.
- Close communication and coordination between affected team members should be encouraged.
- A primary contact or liaison with the audit client should be assigned.

Coordination can be a particular challenge in:

- A large and/or complex audit in which many auditors with different expertise are working independently on different parts of the audit.
- Engagements that involve multiple audit sites, some remote.
- Audits occurring within a global organization where business and cultural practices may vary.

The auditor-in-charge may consider using periodic meetings, in addition to a kickoff meeting, to support communication among audit team members. This can help avoid duplicating effort and can foster sharing of knowledge and experience in solving problems that have arisen. Meetings can be conducted virtually, either in web-assisted meeting platforms or teleconferences.

The auditor-in-charge should examine ways to encourage the right amount of communication among the right team members. Part of the initial team meeting should be devoted to defining:

- What should be communicated to whom.
- When communications should occur.
- What the preferred method of communication is.
- Any legal restrictions on communications.

Secure pages on internal auditing intranet sites can be created so that team members can easily and quickly view each other's work and resources or pose questions.

The auditor-in-charge or delegate may issue regular progress memos or team meeting minutes. These memos can document:

- Assignments.
- Agreements on procedures and approaches.
- Commitments.
- Open issues that require follow-up.

By revisiting minutes at a subsequent meeting, the auditor-in-charge can confirm that open issues have been resolved.

Reviewing Workpapers

Proper supervision of engagements includes reviewing and approving workpapers. This allows the CAE or the delegated supervisor to:

- Be assured that the engagement has been carried out in accordance with high quality standards.
- Evaluate each internal auditor's current skills.
- Identify future development opportunities.

The CAE or delegated supervisor may choose to use a checklist when reviewing workpaper quality. An example of the questions that may be included in the checklist is shown in Exhibit 2-22.

Exhibit 2-22: Example of Workpaper Review Checklist

Test Workpaper Quality Checklist

You can use the following checklist to evaluate testing workpapers:

☐ Is the heading information complete and accurate?

☐ Is the testing objective stated clearly enough that a conclusion can be reached?

☐ Are the sampling and testing methods and the data source described so that someone else could access the same data, re-perform the test, and expect to get the same result?

☐ Are the results detailed enough to provide sufficient evidence to support the conclusion?

☐ Does the summary logically link the results to the conclusion?

☐ Does the testing conclusion directly relate to the testing objective?

☐ If notes are included, are they relevant? Will a future reader of the workpaper understand their relevance?

☐ Are all necessary cross-references, links, and attachments included?

☐ Has all the information been re-checked for accuracy?

☐ Is the workpaper free of typographic errors?

Evidence of conformance with Standard 2340 may include engagement workpapers, either initialed and dated by the engagement supervisor (if documented manually) or electronically approved (if documented in a workpaper software system). Additional evidence may include a completed engagement workpaper review checklist and/or a memorandum of review comments.

If the reviewer has questions about the workpapers, he or she may make a written record—review notes—for the auditor to consider. The workpapers should then include evidence that these questions have been resolved.

Performance Appraisals

Performance appraisal is a process that measures the degree to which an employee accomplishes the work requirements stated in the performance standards and then communicates that information to the employee. It focuses on several levels of performance:

- The entire internal audit activity is assessed on the basis of the annual audit plan and aggregated accomplishments.
- An audit team for a specific engagement can be assessed by both the audit client and the auditor-in-charge.
- Individual auditors can be assessed on a dual schedule. The first track is their performance on specific audits; the second track consists of the annual review by the CAE. The post-audit appraisal can be delivered and discussed immediately following the audit. It can also be aggregated into the discussion at the auditor's annual performance review meeting.

The performance review provides the internal auditor with the opportunity to define his or her professional objectives, cooperate with the manager in designing an action plan to achieve those objectives, and periodically discuss progress and problems related to the plan.

Audit Performance Quality Evidence

Evidence of audit staff performance can be gathered from direct observation and review of an auditor's performance during an audit. Audit managers/supervisors should note and record specific examples of the level of work delivered by individual staff members. Examples of performance may involve observed behaviors and reviews of workpapers.

Evidence may also be gathered from the audit client. An audit effectiveness survey, like the one shown in Exhibit 2-23, can be distributed electronically to audit clients after exit meetings.

Exhibit 2-23: Sample Audit Effectiveness Questionnaire

Customer: _____

Location/function audit: _____

Audit team members: _____

Please evaluate the internal audit recently completed at your location by circling or highlighting the number corresponding to your rating of each performance factor listed below. If you are unable to rate a particular performance factor, simply draw a line through or delete the factor.

	Excellent	Good	Fair	Poor*
SCOPE OF WORK				
1. Timely and clear notification to you of audit purpose and scope	4	3	2	1
2. Inclusion of your concerns and/or suggestions in the audit coverage	4	3	2	1
3. Adequacy of audit coverage on key functions and/or areas	4	3	2	1
PERFORMANCE OF AUDIT WORK				
4. Minimal disruption of normal activities	4	3	2	1
5. Timely communication of audit findings	4	3	2	1
6. Reasonableness and value-added effectiveness of recommendations	4	3	2	1
7. Clarity and objectivity of audit reports	4	3	2	1
8. Consistency of verbal review and written report	4	3	2	1
9. Overall usefulness of the audit to your organization	4	3	2	1

Was there anything about the audit you especially liked or disliked?

_____

_____

* Please provide explanations for any performance factors rated "poor."

_____

_____

How could we have improved the effectiveness of the audit?

_____

_____

Please provide any suggestions for future audits:

_____

_____

Additional comments:

_____

_____

Signature: _____   Date: _____

Please send completed survey to John Doe, Chief Auditing Executive, XYZ, Inc.

v7.0

Post-Audit Review

Post-audit reviews are conducted by the auditor-in-charge for the engagement (along with supervisory or management oversight as deemed appropriate). They generally cover how the engagement went, including:

- Consistency.
- Quality.
- Lessons learned.

Since audit engagements can be so different from one another, the auditor-in-charge may have to develop a unique rating form for each audit—or at least adapt standard forms used in the audit activity. However, criteria would seem to be fairly consistent from audit to audit:

- The quantity of work completed and the ability to stay on schedule and on budget (and proactive communication of anticipated schedule/budget variances, including rationale)

- The quality of the work, including such measures as:
  - Computational accuracy
  - Selection of appropriate tests and the right number of tests
  - Thoroughness in completing all necessary fieldwork tasks
  - Clarity, conciseness, logical organization, professional appearance, and usefulness of workpapers in supporting the final report
  - Quality of written documents and verbal presentations

Post-audit reviews may also be used to help develop individual internal auditors. They should focus separately on job performance issues on the one hand and traits on the other. Traits indicate qualities such as attention to detail, creativity in problem solving, resilience, leadership, judgment, logical thinking, self-confidence, and ability to form and maintain relationships.

The following criteria are examples that may be used during a post-audit review to assess individual auditor performance:

- General grasp of audit procedures and specific understanding of the requirements of the particular engagement
- "People skills," demonstrated in interviews with the audit client's staff and management and with the audit supervisor
- Special technical skills demonstrated on the job, such as ability to perform statistical tests, work with computer-assisted audit programs, create graphic illustrations in a spreadsheet, etc.
- General business knowledge evidenced in understanding the particular challenges faced by the audit client
- Critical thinking skills and insight

Annual Review

The annual review should consider job competencies—the behaviors, abilities, and attributes that can link individuals or teams to enhanced performance and the critical success factors needed to perform the internal auditing role in an organization.

Specific job competencies vary from organization to organization. But many organizations are focusing on the competencies that individuals or audit departments need to perform jobs rather than on specific tasks, duties, knowledge, skills, and responsibilities.

The IIA has released an update to the global competency framework for the internal audit professional, which may be used during an annual review. It consists of four major categories:

- **Professionalism**. Competencies required to demonstrate authority, credibility, and ethical conduct essential for a valuable internal audit activity.

- **Performance**. Competencies required to plan and perform internal audit engagements in conformance with the *Standards*.

- **Environment**. Competencies required to identify and address the risks specific to the industry and environment in which the organization operates.

- **Leadership and Communication**. Competencies required to provide strategic direction, communicate effectively, maintain relationships, and manage internal audit personnel and processes.

Within each of these categories, the competency level may be rated as one of the following:
- General Awareness
- Applied Knowledge
- Expert

The annual performance appraisal with the CAE should include consideration of all the post-audit reviews performed for the internal auditor during the year. The CAE can then provide a more unified viewpoint on the auditor's overall performance, creating continuity in the longer-term action plan for professional development for the auditor.

Face-to-Face Meeting

In addition to documenting the review on a rating form provided to the internal auditor and the CAE, the auditor-in-charge should schedule a face-to-face conference to discuss the ratings with the internal auditor. While these conferences can be approached in different ways, some tactics seem to be generally effective and some seem almost universally ill-advised. The following are some guidelines.

- Schedule the review in advance and be specific about the time it will take and the agenda.

- Open the review in a manner suited to the personalities and relationship of both parties.

- Preface the review with a brief outline of what will be covered, including some indication of the overall ratings. Negative news should be delivered in as objective a manner as possible—without an accusatory or scolding tone of voice.

- Some supervisors ask the person being reviewed to start the conversation with a self-assessment. Note that this should not be done without advance warning.

- Be straightforward during the discussion, whatever the format. The task of the reviewer is to help the auditor develop, and that cannot happen unless reviewer and auditor discuss areas of weakness (or opportunities for improvement/growth) honestly.

- Summarize the review at the end—the positives and the negatives—and gain a commitment from the auditor to take whatever actions have been agreed upon.

Section IV: Communicating Engagement Results and Monitoring Progress

This section is designed to help you:
- Understand preliminary communication with engagement clients.
- Demonstrate qualities of communication: accurate, objective, clear, concise, constructive, complete, and timely.
- Demonstrate communication elements: objectives, scope, conclusions, recommendations, and action plans.
- Deliver interim reporting on engagement process.
- Formulate recommendations to enhance and protect organizational value.
- Describe the audit engagement communication and reporting process.
- Describe the exit conference.
- Describe the development of the audit report, including draft, review, approval, and distribution.
- Describe obtaining management's response.
- Describe the CAE's responsibility for assessing residual risk.
- Describe the process for communicating risk acceptance when management has accepted a level of risk that may be unacceptable to the organization.
- Assess engagement outcomes, including the management action plan.
- Manage monitoring and follow-up of the disposition of audit engagement results communicated to management and the board.

The IIA's guidance referenced in the Learning System may be accessed using the links below. Access to specific pages and documents varies for the public and The IIA members.
- **Attribute Standards:** www.theiia.org/Attribute-standards
- **Performance Standards:** www.theiia.org/Performance-standards
- **Standards and Guidance:** www.theiia.org/Guidance
- **Position Papers:** www.theiia.org/Position-papers
- **Implementation Guidance:** www.theiia.org/Practiceadvisories
- **Practice Guides and GTAGs:** www.theiia.org/Practiceguides

This section of Part 2 focuses on what follows an audit engagement: communicating the results and monitoring for management remediation of audit findings. The results noted in the engagement report have the potential to increase the effectiveness of controls and the management of risk throughout the organization, but only if they are translated by management into actions and if the success of implemented changes is monitored. Internal auditing may facilitate this process of continual organizational improvement by providing specific observations and recommendations, conveying the potential benefits of remedial action, ensuring response to significant risks, and conducting appropriate follow-up and monitoring activities. These tasks can be supported by the development of a culture that recognizes and addresses the obstacles to the remediation of audit findings, the reduction of organizational risk, and the implementation of a system for conducting follow-up.

Chapter 1: Communicating Results and Acceptance of Risk

Effective communication during an engagement—written and verbal, formal and informal—has many dimensions and many benefits:

- **Within the audit team**. Good communication is needed among audit team members to ensure that all aspects of the audit work program are covered and not duplicated. Helpful information must be exchanged as it is learned to improve the quality and efficiency of audit work.

- **With the engagement client**. The audit team and the client must share expectations about the outcomes of the audit and the processes that will be used. Communication can be used to build strong and cooperative relationships with clients and to improve the overall efficiency of the audit. Consistent communication with client management throughout the engagement will minimize the potential for surprises at the conclusion of the audit.

This chapter focuses on the role of communication throughout the engagement process: from initial meetings with clients, to interim or status meetings, to the development and distribution of recommendations and reports.

Topic A: Preliminary Results Communication with Client

This topic discusses the process and considerations for the initial communication of engagement results to engagement clients.

In addition to reviewing the contents of this topic, students can review the following IIA materials:
- Implementation Guidance for 2400 series of *Standards*
- Practice Guide, "Audit Reports: Communicating Assurance Engagement Results"

Preliminary Client Communications

 Performance Standard 2400, "Communicating Results"

Internal auditors must communicate the results of engagements.

The CAE should understand the expectations of the board and senior management regarding communication related to engagement results. Internal auditors must have a clear understanding of engagement communication requirements. Auditors must understand:

- Policies and procedures in the audit manual.
- The use of any standard templates to ensure consistency in developing observations and conclusions.

The internal audit policies and procedures manual establishes the process for documenting support for an observation or conclusion related to the engagement. The internal audit activity may develop an engagement communication plan to provide detailed guidance on how communication will take place during the engagement and how final engagement results will be communicated.

In communicating results, internal auditors must consider the communication plan, including:

- The criteria for communicating (Standard 2410).
- The quality of communication (Standard 2420).
- The dissemination of results (Standard 2440).

These *Standards* are discussed in more detail in the next few topics.

Once it is determined that these *Standards* have been met, the auditor must confirm how the results of the engagement will be communicated. Workpapers will indicate which results will be communicated verbally and which will be communicated in writing.

Conformance with Standard 2400 can be documented by the internal audit policies and procedures manual, which contains:

- Policies regarding the communication of noncompliance with laws, regulations, or other issues.
- Policies for communicating sensitive information within and outside the chain of command.
- Policies for communicating outside the organization.
- Other documentation, for example, a communication plan, observation and escalation records, interim and preliminary communication documents, final engagement communication documents, and monitoring and follow-up communication documents.

Topic B: Communication Elements and Quality

This topic covers the necessary elements for and the importance of high-quality communications.

In addition to reviewing the contents of this topic, students can review the following IIA materials:
- Implementation Guidance for 2410 Series of Standards

Communication Elements

Performance Standard 2410, "Criteria for Communicating"

Communications must include the engagement's objectives, scope, and results.

The format and content of such communications may vary by organization or type of engagement. To ensure that the criteria for communications are met, the internal audit activity must be aware of Standards 2200, 2210, 2220, 2300, 2310, 2320, 2330, and 2340.

Engagement scope and objectives are typically communicated:
- During engagement planning, usually documented in a terms, reference, or engagement letter shared with the client.
- During the engagement, if there are any deviations to the planned scope and objectives.
- In the final engagement communication.

The communication plan typically addresses why, what, to whom, and how internal auditors will communicate. It may also specify the use of a particular communication format. The plan is typically discussed with relevant stakeholders in advance of any engagement fieldwork.

When planning the final engagement communications, all relevant workpapers and workpaper summaries will be considered as well as:
- Stakeholder expectations.
- Engagement objectives.
- Strategic goals of the area under review.
- Scope of the engagement and any scope limitations.
- Engagement results.

Implementation Standard 2410.A1 (Assurance Engagements)

Final communication of engagement results must include applicable conclusions, as well as applicable recommendations and/or action plans. Where appropriate, the internal auditors' opinion should be provided. An opinion must take into account the expectations of senior management, the board, and other stakeholders and must be supported by sufficient, reliable, relevant, and useful information.

Applicable conclusions and recommendations and/or action plans may include a rating, conclusion, or other description of the results and their significance.

Implementation Standard 2410.A2 (Assurance Engagements)

Internal auditors are encouraged to acknowledge satisfactory performance in engagement communications.

Communication with management is an ongoing process, and the internal audit activity adds value by developing communications that effect positive change in the organization. As illustrated by Standard 2410.A2, positive change may be promoted by acknowledging satisfactory performance.

Implementation Standard 2410.A3 (Assurance Engagements)

When releasing engagement results to parties outside the organization, the communication must include limitations on distribution and use of the results.

Conformance may be demonstrated via:
- Written internal audit activity policies that address the consistency of the engagement report format.
- Any materials that demonstrate how the communication plan was developed.
- Adherence to:
  - The communication plan.
  - Written reports.
  - Engagement letters.

Implementation Standard 2410.C1 (Consulting Engagements)

Communication of the progress and results of consulting engagements will vary in form and content depending upon the nature of the engagement and the needs of the client.

Due to the nature of consulting engagements, the communication methods and criteria will be highly variable from engagement to engagement and client to client, as indicated by Standard 2410.C1.

Report Elements

The format and content of the engagement's final conclusions may vary with the type of organization and engagement but nevertheless must include the engagement's objectives, scope, and results, including applicable conclusions and recommendations and/or action plans.

- **Objectives of the engagement.** A precise statement of the objectives of the engagement can provide coherence to the rest of the report and make it easier to read and discuss. The audit findings should always be related to the audit's objectives.

- **Scope of the engagement.** The scope statement identifies the activities audited. It may also specify activities excluded from the audit, if the title of the audit would naturally lead readers to expect to find coverage of those activities. The scope statement may include the time period reviewed, and it may be combined with the objectives.

- **Audit methods.** This may or may not be a separate section. A separate section is often merited if new methodologies or new technology is being used or if the work of other bodies (internal or external) provides a substantial basis for the engagement. In place of a separate section, the report may include a section on relevant methodology in the discussion of each observation.

- **Results.** The results section should include observations, conclusions, opinions, recommendations, and action plans. Some complex reports may be preceded by an observations summary, perhaps in a table format that identifies and describes specific observations that will be discussed in the body of the report. Minor observations may be put in a separate section. The recommendations may also be in a separate section if they are general and not tied to specific observations.

Where appropriate, the auditor's opinion should be provided.

Final communications may include other optional sections:

- **Background information.** Background information may describe the organization and the activities to be reviewed along with the results and status of previous audits of the same activities.

- **Summaries.** A summary can be a useful memorandum accompanying the full report when it is provided to an executive in the organization.

- **Client accomplishments.** The final communication may include descriptions of improvements the client has made in response to a previous audit.

- **Client views.** The report may include the client's views on the engagement's conclusions and recommendations. Disagreements between the client and the internal audit activity may require intervention from an executive. The client's written comments may be included in an appendix or cover letter.

The final presentation to the client does not require a written document. Many auditors present their conclusions and recommendations in a slide presentation.

The report should be signed by the CAE or an audit activity team member authorized to do so by the CAE. A signed version of the report should be kept on file by the internal audit activity.

Exhibit 2-24 contains an example of a format for an audit report. Note that there will likely be multiple sections containing observations, each with their own description, cause, etc.

Exhibit 2-24: Audit Report Template

Reference	(A.2) Bank Account Access Controls Lacking
Criticality	**Significant**

Observation

Control deficiencies were identified related to bank account access as follows:

Terminations of employment and position transfers for users with bank account access are not communicated to bank account security administrators as 20.9% (9 out of 43) of users with bank account access were terminated or transferred without adjustments being made to their account access privileges. A user was also given access to generate reports for a bank account the user had no business reason to access.

Additionally, it is not currently the practice of ABC Unlimited to recover the bank access account tokens upon termination of employment or transfer to a new position. This combination of factors could result in unauthorized access to company accounts as terminated associates or associates transferring to new positions retain both the system login credentials and bank access token required to access company accounts.

While the accounts where terminated or transferred associates retained access were not accounts where company funds could be directly funneled outside the organization, those with access could process unauthorized fund pulls from customer accounts. This could result in losing customer accounts and reduced customer confidence in the organization.

Recommendation

Management should establish a process where Treasury is notified immediately when associates with bank account access are terminated or transferred to new positions within the organization. This will help reduce the risk of unauthorized account access and will aid Treasury in maintaining bank access entitlements.

A review of the bank access entitlements of all users should be performed annually.

Planned action

Management agrees there needs to be greater communication between Treasury, Credit and Human Resources to ensure that all employees with banking access are current employees with roles in the AR/Credit area. Treasury will establish a one over one (preparer and approver) control process to review current users on a quarterly basis and will establish a practice of turning over their token ID to their supervisor at their respective location.

Responsible	Miguel Money, Controller
Target date	30 June 20XX
Latest update	

Source: Practice Guide "Audit Reports: Communicating Assurance Engagement Results"

Communication Quality

Performance Standard 2420, "Quality of Communications"

Communications must be accurate, objective, clear, concise, constructive, complete, and timely.

- **Accurate** communications are free from errors and distortions and are faithful to the underlying facts.
  - Precise wording supported by evidence gathered during the engagement is important.
  - Auditors must "disclose all material facts known to them that, if not disclosed, may distort the reporting of activities under review" per The IIA's Code of Ethics.
  - If an error occurs, the CAE must communicate the corrected information per Standard 2421.

- **Objective** communications are fair, impartial, and unbiased and are the result of a fair-minded and balanced assessment of all relevant facts and circumstances.
  - Unbiased phrasing and a focus on deficiencies in processes and their execution helps ensure objectivity.
  - Objectivity starts with the unbiased mental attitude that auditors should possess when performing engagements.

- **Clear** communications are easily understood and logical, avoiding unnecessary technical language.
  - Clarity is increased by using language that is easily understood and is consistent with terminology used in the industry and by the organization.
  - It is also enhanced when auditors communicate important observations and findings and logically support recommendations and conclusions for a particular engagement.

- **Concise** communications are to the point and avoid unnecessary elaboration, superfluous detail, redundancy, and wordiness.
  - Exclude information that is unnecessary, insignificant, or unrelated to the engagement.

- **Constructive** communications are helpful to the engagement client and the organization and lead to improvements where needed.
  - It is helpful to use a constructive tone throughout the communication that reflects the severity of observations.
  - Constructive communications enable a collaborative process for determining solutions that facilitate positive change.

- **Complete** communications contain everything that is essential to the target audience and all significant and relevant information to support recommendations and conclusions.
  - Auditors should consider any information that is essential to the target audience.

- **Timely** communications are opportune and expedient, depending on the significance of the issue.
  - All communications should be submitted by the deadlines established during the planning phase.
  - Timeliness may vary by organization and may be determined by benchmarking and conducting research relative to the engagement subject.

Topic C: Interim Reporting

This topic discusses the benefits and importance of communication during the engagement process and how communication throughout the engagement improves outcomes and enhances final communications.

In addition to reviewing the contents of this topic, students can review the following IIA materials:
- Implementation Guidance on 2420 Series of Standards

Preparing Interim Reporting

Communication with management is an ongoing process throughout the engagement. The internal audit activity adds value by developing communications that effect positive change in the organization.

Internal auditors should communicate with process owners and managers during:
- Engagement planning.
- Fieldwork.
- Testing.

Interim reports may be used to:
- Communicate information that requires immediate attention.
- Communicate a change in the engagement objectives.
- Communicate a change in engagement scope for the activity under review.
- Keep management informed of engagement progress when engagements extend over a long period of time.

Another reason for interim communications is to inform management of significant matters not related to the engagement.

Interim reports may be:
- Written.
- Verbal.
- Transmitted formally.
- Transmitted informally.

Interim progress can be reported through a status meeting, report, or email. The point is that ongoing communication should be maintained throughout the audit engagement.

Communicating observations on an interim basis has advantages:

- The engagement process becomes more efficient, as auditors can clarify issues before unnecessary work is performed.

- The engagement process is more effective, since interim informal meetings help ensure that relevant information is uncovered and understood before evaluations are made and recommendations formulated.

- Auditor-client relationships are strengthened.

The use of interim reports does not diminish or eliminate the need for a final engagement communication. Interim written reports can:
- Be a path to higher-quality final reports.
- Lead to more client buy-in.
- Result in increased detail in reports.
- Reduce the time needed to create a draft final report.

Findings in the interim report may be excluded from the final report if they have been properly resolved and are no longer of importance to the client's operations.

Topic D: Recommendations to Enhance and Protect Value

This topic discusses the internal audit activity focus on creating and protecting value for the organization through engagement procedures.

In addition to reviewing the contents of this topic, students can review the following IIA materials:
- Implementation Guidance for Standard 2320

Forming Value Recommendations

In accordance with Standard 2410.A1, the final communication of engagement results must include applicable:

- Conclusions.
- Recommendations.
- Action plans.

This communication:

- Provides an opportunity to have a dialogue regarding the value the board and senior management receive from the audited activities.
- Allows for identification of additional value-adding activities the internal audit function can engage in to maximize the overall value it can provide the organization.

Consulting and advisory services provide value only if their recommendations to senior management contain information that senior management would not otherwise have. Internal auditors should have a strong awareness of the strategic objectives of the organization so that the consulting services they provide truly add value.

What's in a Recommendation?

Internal auditors must document information that logically supports the engagement results and conclusions. Effective workpapers contain information that is sufficient and relevant to the engagement:

- Objectives
- Observations
- Conclusions
- Recommendations

This makes the information useful in helping the organization meet its goals.

The following is some specific guidance about recommendations:

- Recommendations are based on the internal auditor's observations and conclusions.
- Recommendations call for action to correct existing conditions or to improve operations, and they may suggest approaches to correcting or enhancing performance as a guide for management in achieving desired results.
- Recommendations can be general or specific. For example, under some circumstances, the internal auditor may recommend a general course of action and specific suggestions for implementation. In other circumstances, the internal auditor may suggest further investigation or study.

An effective approach to developing recommendations is to adhere to the **SMART** principle shown in Exhibit 2-25.

Exhibit 2-25: SMART Model for Composing Recommendations

S	Specific
M	Measurable
A	Action-oriented
R	Relevant
T	Time-based

- **Specific** recommendations outline exactly what the organization should aim to accomplish.
- **Measurable** recommendations can be evaluated to determine whether they have been accomplished.
- **Action-oriented** recommendations specify the actions that the organization will be able to take.
- **Relevant** recommendations relate to the nature of the organization, and they are attainable.
- **Time-based** recommendations specify the time frame for accomplishing the recommendations.

The internal auditor should go through a logical, thorough process and analyze the recommendations before incorporating them into an engagement communication.

Basic considerations include but are not limited to the following:
- Does the recommendation add value?
- Will it address the root cause?
- Are the costs realistic in terms of the expected benefits?

Internal auditors should maintain their objectivity when drawing conclusions and offering advice to management. Any impairments that existed prior to the engagement or that develop during it should be disclosed to management immediately.

Recommendations are not commands, merely options, and the auditor should not deliver a recommendation as if it were the only possible course of action, because the manager generally has a broader view of the possible consequences of acting upon a recommendation than the auditor.

It's a good idea to bring recommendations to the manager for discussion before the end of the audit. Working jointly with the manager to come to agreement about a course of corrective action improves the relationship. The manager will look better to superiors if the audit report states that recommendations were developed after discussion with the manager.

The internal auditor should consider the relationship between the cost of a recommended action and the benefit to the organization. Some actions must be taken regardless of cost to bring the organization into compliance with a law or regulation, but otherwise there should be a balance between cost and risk.

Topic E: Engagement Communication and Reporting Process

This topic covers the communication and reporting process for engagements, including exit conferences, the process for developing the audit report, and how to obtain management's response.

In addition to reviewing the contents of this topic, students can review the following IIA materials:
- Implementation Guidance for 2440 Series of Standards

Engagement Communication and Reporting Process

Performance Standard 2440, "Disseminating Results"

The chief audit executive must communicate results to the appropriate parties.

The CAE is responsible for reviewing and approving the final engagement communication before issuance and for deciding to whom and how it will be disseminated.

The CAE typically will use the following when determining whom to communicate results to and what form they should take:
- An understanding of organizational communication protocols
- An understanding of the organization chart
- Discussions with the board

The audit charter and the communication protocols of the organization may help the CAE determine the process for reporting outside the organization. Considerations would include factors such as which parties to address in the final communication or which parties should receive copies of it and when to notify regulators who oversee the organization's industry.

To ensure compliance with legal obligations and organizational protocols, the CAE should take great care and consideration when preparing to disseminate results outside the organization. This includes considering the ramifications of communicating sensitive information. It may be helpful to consult with legal counsel and compliance areas within the organization.

When determining the recipients of the report, the CAE may take into consideration whether any parties have:
- A business need for receiving the results.
- Any responsibility for management action plans.

To ensure consistency, the internal audit activity may develop:
- A standard distribution list of parties who receive all communications.
- Management levels that should be included on a distribution list for engagement results pertaining to their area of responsibility.

Results may be communicated verbally or in writing, and the format may differ depending on the recipient.

Authority for implementing Standard 2440 may be delegated, but the responsibility cannot be delegated.

The CAE can demonstrate conformance by:
- Verifying the level of review and ensuring sign-off on all workpapers before issuing the final communication.
- Retaining copies of written communication.
- Maintaining evidence of the verbal communication of others through:
  - Meeting minutes.
  - Presentations.
  - Memos that identify attendees receiving the communication.

Maintaining a complete list of internal audit engagement results is important in the event that an error or omission is identified after the dissemination of results.

Performance Standard 2421, "Errors and Omissions"

If a final communication contains a significant error or omission, the chief audit executive must communicate corrected information to all parties who received the original communication.

The CAE must understand the expectations of the board and senior management regarding which errors or omissions they would consider significant.

If the CAE becomes aware of an error, he or she can determine its significance on the basis of the following questions:
- Would the error or omission change the results of the engagement?
- Would the error or omission change someone's mind about the severity of the findings?

- Would the error or omission change a conclusion?
- Would the error or omission change an opinion?
- Would the error or omission change a recommended action?

If the CAE determines that an error is significant, he or she must determine the best way to communicate the error in a way that will reach all parties who received the original communication.

Conformance with Standard 2421 can be demonstrated by:
- The existence of internal audit policies and procedures for handling errors and omissions.
- Email correspondence and other records documenting how the CAE determined the significance and cause of the error or omission.
- Evidentiary materials showing the specific information that was communicated as well as how and when it was communicated.

Developing the Audit Report

The steps in developing the audit report include drafting, reviewing, approving, and distributing it.

Drafting

When drafting the audit report, it is important to keep the needs of the audience in mind.
- If there will be more than one audience, there may (or may not) need to be more than one version of the report.
- If different versions of the report are deemed beneficial, it is imperative that the overall objective substance of the report (e.g., final results, opinions, issues/recommendations, management responses) be unchanged between the versions.

Report drafting needs to be a timely endeavor, and a good way to ensure that this occurs is to create deadlines for each draft and its review.

It is important to follow some basic writing principles when drafting a report. This can include creating an outline and then two or three drafts of the report.
- An outline indicates what you will discuss and in what order. For example, it could list the headings or slide titles and then include brief summaries of what each will contain. Outlining before writing can prevent the inclusion of things that could be omitted.
- The first draft will involve getting the information down—the hard work of summarizing audit work and findings, formatting charts for presentation, and so on.
- The second and third drafts can then focus on cleaning up the writing, improving the organization of the materials for logical flow, and ensuring that points are clear, concise, and provided in a constructive tone and that good mechanics are used overall.

Reviewing

Having someone who did not write the outline and drafts read and comment on the report at each stage of its development can help show areas that are confusing, incomplete, have flaws in logic, and so on. Options may include:

- A supervisor.
- Audit clients.

In selecting a reviewer, internal auditors need to consider who should have access to the sensitive contents of the report.

In addition to reviewing to improve grammar and style, reviewers should look for whether:

- The report is factually correct.
- The report is complete.
- Conclusions are supported by evidence that is sufficient, reliable, relevant, and useful.

A few areas of the report are especially important to review for proper tone. One of these is the discussion of management's action plans. It is important to emphasize an expected completion time line and sufficient urgency, but it is also important to ensure that the tone is constructive. Matters of lower significance should not be made to seem more important than they actually are, so that areas of high significance will stand out.

Approving

The CAE or a designee should review and approve the final engagement communication before it is issued and should decide who will receive it.

The CAE may authorize the following personnel to sign engagement reports on the CAE's behalf:

- Auditor-in-charge
- Audit supervisor
- Lead auditor

In large international organizations, requiring the CAE's signature on all final communications might cause delays.

Even when another person is authorized to sign the engagement reports, the CAE maintains responsibility for communicating the final results of an engagement in accordance with Performance Standard 2440, "Disseminating Results."

Distributing

The CAE bears responsibility for communicating final results to individuals who can ensure that the results are given due consideration. The report should go to those in positions to take corrective action—for example, management of the audited area or operation, senior management, or associated functions that may be affected by or can support recommended action plans.

Communications may also go to external auditors, the board, and others who are affected by or interested in the results.

If substantive corrections must be made to a report after it has been distributed, the CAE should issue a new report that highlights the changes and see that is distributed to all recipients of the original report.

Before releasing reports to parties outside the organization, the CAE should:
* Assess potential risks to the organization.
* Obtain approval of senior management, legal counsel, or both.

The CAE is responsible for controlling the distribution of the report.

Release of consulting reports should be consistent with the organization's established practices. Because of the nature of the activities that internal auditing helps to evaluate, many organizations allow only limited distribution of consulting reports.

Holding the Exit Conference

The final act of an audit engagement is communicating its results—the findings and recommendations. The discussion here focuses on written audit reports, but the communication may be in other formats: verbal, web-based, or a slide presentation.

The CAE bears responsibility for seeing that the final report is:
* Skillfully prepared.
* Adroitly presented.
* Brought to the attention of the client's decision makers.
* Kept out of the hands of those who are not authorized to receive it.

Chances for a favorable reception of the audit report can be improved if client managers have been consulted about the findings and recommendations before communication of the final draft. It helps to have key people on your side when you deliver the recommendations.

After creation of a rough draft of the final report, there should be a meeting between the process owners (the audit clients) and the internal auditing team. This is generally called the **exit conference**, exit interview, or post-engagement meeting. People attending the exit conference are often the same participants who attended the entrance conference, including people:

- Familiar with operations details.
- Who can authorize the implementation of corrective actions.

The objectives of the exit conference include:

- Discussing conclusions and recommendations.
- Resolving any misunderstandings or misinterpretations of fact by allowing the client to ask for clarification of specific items and to express views on observations, conclusions, and recommendations.
- Reaching agreement on possible solutions to problems identified in the report. This can help the management of the area to formulate its response to the audit findings, which may require requesting budget or making or changing policies.
- Expressing appreciation for cooperation during the performance of the internal audit and for providing required information in a timely fashion.

The IIA seminar "Tools and Techniques I: New Internal Auditor" recommends the following best practices for the logistics of exit conferences:

- Ensure that the right people attend.
- Provide the necessary documents (i.e., the draft report) in advance.
- Set the agenda and manage the meeting.
- Explore and resolve as many issues as possible.
- Provide clear messages, even about difficult issues.
- Thank the audit customer for cooperation, both at the beginning and the end of the conference, acknowledging the key contacts by name and recognizing that audits can be disruptive to normal activities.
- Hold a post-meeting debriefing with the audit team.

Management's Response

It can be advantageous for the CAE to review the draft engagement communications before communicating the results, as it may be appropriate for results to be delivered via a meeting with a presentation and an opportunity for discussion. This is because once the final report has been completed and distributed, the chance for serious dialogue on the findings may have passed.

When planning the final engagement communication, internal auditors should consider any discussions and interim communications they have had with the management of the area under review. At this stage, the client can clear up misunderstandings and react to the findings while there is time to collaborate on revisions.

The participants in these discussions will generally be individuals who are knowledgeable about the detailed operations and those who can authorize the implementation of corrective action.

In other words, if you can get early agreement on the recommendations from the people who can effect changes in the client's operations, you have a much better chance of getting the final report acted upon.

Topic F: CAE's Assessment of Residual Risk

This topic describes the requirements for the CAE to assess residual risk following the communication of audit engagement results.

In addition to reviewing the contents of this topic, students can review the following IIA materials:
- Implementation Guidance for Standard 2600

CAE's Responsibility for Assessing Residual Risk

Performance Standard 2600, "Communicating the Acceptance of Risks"

When the chief audit executive concludes that management has accepted a level of risk that may be unacceptable to the organization, the chief audit executive must discuss the matter with senior management. If the chief audit executive determines that the matter has not been resolved, the chief audit executive must communicate the matter to the board.

Standard 2600 addresses the issue of accepting a level of residual risk that may be unacceptable to the organization. **Residual risk** is the portion of inherent risk that remains after management executes its risk responses. When the CAE concludes that management has accepted a level of risk that is unacceptable, the CAE must address the issue with senior management and then the board, if necessary.

Residual risk may be found:
- Through an assurance or consulting engagement.
- By monitoring the actions taken by management on prior engagement results.
- By other means.

The CAE is not responsible for resolving the risk.

In order to be successful, the CAE must understand the organization's tolerance for various types of organizational risks. If the organization has a formal risk management policy, which may include a risk acceptance policy, the CAE and the internal audit activity must understand it. Highly significant risks may include:

- Those that may harm the organization's reputation.
- Those that could harm people.
- Those that would result in significant regulatory fines, limitations on business conduct, or other financial or contractual penalties.
- Material misstatements.
- Fraud or other illegal acts.
- Significant impediments to achieving strategic objectives.

The CAE may identify high-risk observations that are not corrected in a timely manner through monitoring the disposition of results and associated corrective actions, but ongoing monitoring is not the only way to identify unacceptable risk.

Topic G: Communicating Risk Acceptance

This topic covers what the CAE should do when he or she determines that senior management is accepting a level of risk that is unacceptable to the organization.

In addition to reviewing the contents of this topic, students can review the following IIA materials:
- Implementation Guidance for Standard 2600

Risk Acceptance Communication Process

To effectively carry out the intent of Standard 2600, several things are necessary:

- The CAE must have access to senior management and the board in order to be able to communicate and discuss his or her point of view in a timely manner.
- The CAE must be able to identify whether there are areas of unacceptable risk.
- The CAE must demonstrate strong management and communication skills to professionally navigate the communication process with senior management and the board.

In order to communicate risk acceptance through the proper channels, it is helpful for the CAE to know how higher-risk issues are typically communicated within the organization.

If the CAE recognizes that the risk level is higher than is tolerable and is not being acceptably mitigated, he or she is required to communicate the situation to senior management and later to the board if senior management does not resolve the risk acceptably. Prior to this communication, the CAE typically discusses the issue with members of management responsible for the risk area.

The CAE uses judgment to determine how best and how quickly to communicate such matters and to whom, based on:

- The issue's nature.
- The issue's urgency.
- Potential ramifications.
- Any policies that may be in place.

Evidence of conformance with Standard 2600 can be found in:

- The minutes of meetings where a significant risk issue was discussed with the executive management team, the board, or a risk committee.
- A memo regarding private conversations or one-on-one meetings.

Chapter 2: Monitoring Progress

Internal auditing assurance or consulting engagements are discrete projects that use project management approaches during planning and execution. A risk of project-based work is that no one will follow up on management action plans documented in the final audit report because the team members have moved on to the next project and have other responsibilities, deadlines, and time constraints. However, if this natural tendency is allowed to occur or persist, it can create a more significant risk for the internal audit activity. The activity could be perceived as irrelevant and not value-added because no real changes are being made and no improvements in results are being realized. The entire internal control framework could be jeopardized if management falls into a routine of ignoring audit recommendations and fails to properly execute its control monitoring responsibilities.

Monitoring of engagement outcomes is not just a minor afterthought but a critical control step that needs to be championed to the board, senior management, and process owners; included in the annual audit plan and personnel schedules; and assigned to specific personnel who are held responsible and accountable. (Note that in a consulting project, monitoring is performed only if it was an objective requested by management.)

This decision can be to implement all or some of the recommendations or to accept the risk and do nothing. The decision should have been arrived at in collaboration with internal auditing, so the CAE should support the method used. If not, the CAE should escalate the issue to the board or senior management.

This chapter starts by looking at the assessment of engagement outcomes. Internal auditors will typically decide on the most appropriate monitoring method in consultation with the manager responsible for implementing the action plan. Internal auditors document the process to be used in the final engagement report. The remainder of the chapter shows how to execute this follow-up process and report adequate or inadequate actions to the board or management.

Topic A: Outcomes and Action Plans

This topic discusses the CAE's responsibility for monitoring the disposition of results following their communication to stakeholders.

In addition to reviewing the contents of this topic, students can review the following IIA materials:
• Implementation Guidance for Standard 2500

Outcomes and Management Action Plans

Performance Standard 2500, "Monitoring Progress"
The chief audit executive must establish and maintain a system to monitor the disposition of results communicated to management.

The CAE should start by attaining a clear understanding of the type of information and the level of detail the board and senior management expect with regard to the internal audit activity's monitoring of the results of engagements.

Periodic interactions with management responsible for implementing corrective actions will be required, so it is generally helpful to solicit management's input on ways to create an effective monitoring process.

The CAE may want to benchmark with other CAEs or compliance functions that monitor outstanding issues to identify leading practices that have proven effective.

Monitoring processes may vary in complexity depending on a number of factors. However the monitoring process is executed, it must capture relevant observations, agreed corrective action, and current status. Typically tracked and captured information includes:
• The observations communicated to management and their relative risk rating.
• The nature of the agreed corrective actions.
• The timing/deadlines/age of the corrective actions and changes in target dates.
• The management/process owner responsible for each corrective action.
• The current status of corrective actions and whether the internal audit has confirmed the status.

The CAE may develop or purchase a tool, mechanism, or system to track, monitor, and report on such information.

Key Point

Certain reported observations and recommendations may be so significant that they require immediate action by management. In such situations, internal audit should monitor these conditions until corrected because of the effect they may have on the organization.

The CAE's professional judgment and expectations set by the board are used to determine the:

- Frequency of monitoring.
- Approach to monitoring.
- Form of reporting.

Conformance is evidenced by the existence of a routinely updated exception tracking system or by corrective action status reports prepared for senior management and the board.

Topic B: Monitoring and Follow-up

This topic discusses the responsibilities of internal audit following the distribution of engagement results, including the timing and manner of follow-up procedures.

Monitoring and Follow-Up

The IIA

Implementation Standard 2500.A1 (Assurance Engagements)

The chief audit executive must establish a follow-up process to monitor and ensure that management actions have been effectively implemented or that senior management has accepted the risk of not taking action.

The internal audit function's responsibilities do not end when engagement results are distributed. Monitoring and follow-up procedures are designed to ensure that observations have been addressed and resolved in a manner consistent with management's response included in the final engagement communication.

During consulting engagements, follow-up monitoring procedures will be dictated by the agreement with the client, as indicated by Standard 2500.C1.

The IIA

Implementation Standard 2500.C1 (Consulting Engagements)

The internal audit activity must monitor the disposition of results of consulting engagements to the extent agreed upon with the client.

Factors that might be considered when determining appropriate follow-up procedures are:
- Significance of the reported observation or recommendation.
- Degree of effort and cost needed to correct the reported condition.
- Impacts that may result should the corrective action fail.
- Complexity of the corrective action.
- Time period involved.

A best practice is for the CAE to schedule follow-up activities as part of the development of engagement work schedules.

Following up includes confirming with the client that corrective action has been implemented and performing appropriate retesting procedures to ensure that the risk is mitigated.

An observation is not considered remediated until retesting confirms that:
- Implemented controls are designed and operating effectively.
- The associated risk is mitigated to acceptable levels.

Typically, reporting to senior management or the audit committee and independent outside auditors over open observations occurs at least quarterly.

If management chooses to accept a risk, the CAE must:
- Make a judgment regarding the prudence of the decision.
- Report it to senior management and/or the board if he or she judges the level of risk to be unacceptable to the organization.

If management accepts responsibility for implementing changes to remediate the observations, the internal audit function must monitor the progress that management makes. Regular follow-up procedures should ensure that the enhancements are made on schedule with the time frame outlined in the final engagement communication.

The process for establishing and maintaining a system to monitor the disposition of audit engagement results should be delineated in the internal audit function's audit manual. Follow-up actions should be documented and retained in workpapers.

This page intentionally left blank.

Bibliography

The following references were used in the development of Part 2 of The IIA's CIA Learning System. Please note that all website references were valid as of April 2020.

Anderson, Urton, and Andrew J. Dahle. *Applying the International Professional Practices Framework,* fourth edition. Lake Mary, Florida: The Institute of Internal Auditors, 2018.

"The Audit Committee: Purpose, Process, Professionalism." The Institute of Internal Auditors, www.yumpu.com/en/document/view/36619613/the-audit-committee-purpose-process-professionalism.

"Audit Reports: Communicating Assurance Engagement Results" (IPPF Practice Guide). Altamonte Springs, Florida: The Institute of Internal Auditors, 2009.

"Auditing External Business Relationships" (IPPF Practice Guide). Altamonte Springs, Florida: The Institute of Internal Auditors, 2009.

"Auditing Techniques" course. Altamonte Springs, Florida: The Institute of Internal Auditors.

Committee of Sponsoring Organizations of the Treadway Commission. *Enterprise Risk Management—Integrating with Strategy and Performance.* Jersey City, New Jersey: American Institute of Certified Public Accountants, 2017.

Committee of Sponsoring Organizations of the Treadway Commission. *Guidance on Monitoring Internal Control Systems.* Jersey City, New Jersey: American Institute of Certified Public Accountants, 2009.

Committee of Sponsoring Organizations of the Treadway Commission. *Internal Control—Integrated Framework.* Jersey City, New Jersey: American Institute of Certified Public Accountants, 1994.

Committee of Sponsoring Organizations of the Treadway Commission. *Internal Control—Integrated Framework (2013).* Jersey City, New Jersey: American Institute of Certified Public Accountants, 2013.

Committee of Sponsoring Organizations of the Treadway Commission and World Business Council for Sustainable Development. "Enterprise Risk Management—Applying Enterprise Risk Management to Environmental, Social and Governance-Related Risks." docs.wbcsd.org/2018/10/COSO_WBCSD_ESGERM_Guidance.pdf.

"Comparison of SOC 1, SOC 2 and SOC 3 Reports." AICPA, competency.aicpa.org/media_resources/208716-comparison-of-soc-1-soc-2-and-soc-3-reports.

"Continuous Auditing: Coordinating Continuous Auditing and Monitoring to Provide Continuous Assurance, 2nd Edition(Global Technology Audit Guide [GTAG] 3). The Institute of Internal Auditors, 2015.

"Coordination and Reliance: Developing an Assurance Map" (IPPF Practice Guide). Lake Mary, Florida: The Institute of Internal Auditors, 2017.

"Difference Between GDPR and ePrivacy Regulation." PrivacyTrust, www.privacytrust.com/guidance/gdpr-vs-eprivacy-regulation.html.

"Effective Writing for Auditors" seminar. Altamonte Springs, Florida: The Institute of Internal Auditors.

"Engagement Planning: Assessing Fraud Risks" (IPPF Practice Guide). Lake Mary, Florida: The Institute of Internal Auditors, 2017.

"Engagement Planning: Establishing Objectives and Scope" (IPPF Practice Guide). Lake Mary, Florida: The Institute of Internal Auditors, 2017.

"Formulating and Expressing Internal Audit Opinions" (IPPF Practice Guide). Altamonte Springs, Florida: The Institute of Internal Auditors, 2009.

"Gramm-Leach-Bliley Act." Federal Trade Commission, www.ftc.gov/tips-advice/business-center/privacy-and-security/gramm-leach-bliley-act.

Hargraves, Kim, et al. *Privacy: Assessing the Risk.* Altamonte Springs, Florida: Institute of Internal Auditors Research Foundation, 2003.

Hornreich, Jaike. "Understanding the New SSAE 18—What You Need to Know." Skoda Minotti, skodaminotti.com/blog/understanding-new-ssae-18-need-know/, April 12, 2017.

Hubbard, Larry. *Control Self-Assessment: A Practical Guide.* Altamonte Springs, Florida: The Institute of Internal Auditors, 2000.

"Interaction with the Board" (IPPF Practice Guide). Alamonte Springs, Florida: The Institute of Internal Auditors, 2011.

Internal Audit Foundation. *Sawyer's Internal Auditing,* seventh edition. Lake Mary, Florida: Internal Audit Foundation, 2019.

Jerskey, Pamela. "Automated Workpapers Made Easy."

Mautz, Robert K. *Internal Control in U.S. Corporations: The State of the Art.* New York: Financial Executives Research Foundation, 1980.

"Measuring Internal Audit Effectiveness and Efficiency" (IPPF Practice Guide). Altamonte Springs, Florida: The Institute of Internal Auditors, 2010.

Reding, Kurt F., et al. *Internal Auditing: Assurance and Consulting Services.* Altamonte Springs, Florida: The Institute of Internal Auditors Research Foundation, 2009.

Sawyer, Lawrence B., Mortimer A. Dittenhofer, and James H. Scheiner. *Sawyer's Internal Auditing,* fifth edition. Altamonte Springs, Florida: The Institute of Internal Auditors, 2005.

Six Sigma Material. www.six-sigma-material.com/Spaghetti-Diagram.html, 2018.

"Software Directory." The Institute of Internal Auditors Australia, www.iia.org.au/technical-resources/software-directory.

Thomas, Archie R. *Essentials: An Internal Audit Operations Manual.* Altamonte Springs, Florida: The Institute of Internal Auditors Research Foundation, 2008.

"Tools and Techniques I: New Internal Auditor" seminar. Lake Mary, Florida: The Institute of Internal Auditors.

U.S. General Accounting Office. "How to Get Action on Audit Recommendations." U.S. General Accounting Office, www.gao.gov/special.pubs/p0921.pdf.

World Economic Forum. "The Global Risks Report 2018." World Economic Forum, www.weforum.org/reports/the-global-risks-report-2018.

Zhang, Charles. "The Art of Coordination." *Internal Auditor,* April 1998, Volume 55, Issue 2.

This page intentionally left blank.

Index

A

acceptance of risk, 2-145
advisory consulting engagements, 2-30
analytical reviews, 2-96, 2-97
annual performance review, 2-124
assurance engagements, 2-15
assurance maps, 2-14
attributes sampling, 2-77
audit documentation, 2-68
audit plans, 2-9, 2-39, 2-40
audit policies, 2-4, 2-5
audit procedures, 2-5
audit reports, 2-131, 2-138, 2-140
audit universe, 2-10
auditable units, 2-10
audits
    compliance, 2-20
    due diligence, 2-28, 2-30
    of external business relationships, 2-22
    financial/financial reporting, 2-18
    operational, 2-16
    performance, 2-21
    privacy, 2-25, 2-30
    quality, 2-27
    security, 2-17
    See Also engagements

B

benchmarking, 2-30
blended engagements, 2-30
block diagrams, 2-92
budgets, 2-63, 2-98
business process mapping, 2-30

C

CAATs (computer-assisted auditing techniques), 2-66, 2-82
cause, in findings, 2-113
cause-and-effect diagrams, 2-102
checklists, 2-73, 2-74
communication, 2-118
    with board/senior management, 2-39, 2-40
    elements of, 2-129
    with engagement client, 2-128, 2-134, 2-138
    quality, 2-133

compliance audits, 2-20
computer-assisted auditing techniques, 2-66, 2-82
conclusions, 2-113
condition, in findings, 2-113
confirmation, 2-68
consequence, in findings, 2-113
consulting engagements, 2-30
control self-assessments, 2-30
controls, assessing adequacy/effectiveness, 2-111
coordination with other audit/oversight entities, 2-36, 2-37
corrective action, 2-113
corroborative evidence, 2-84
criteria, 2-52, 2-113
CSAs (control self-assessments), 2-30

D

data
    analysis, 2-86
    evaluation, 2-86
    gathering, 2-66
discovery sampling, 2-77
due diligence audits, 2-28, 2-30

E

engagements
    assurance, 2-15
    blended, 2-30
    communicating results, 2-111
    conclusions, 2-111, 2-113
    consulting, 2-30
    criteria, 2-52
    findings, 2-113
    follow-up, 2-148
    monitoring progress, 2-148
    objectives, 2-48
    observations, 2-112
    opinions, 2-114
    outcomes, assessing, 2-147
    planning, 2-48, 2-55
    prioritization of, 2-14
    procedures, 2-62
    recommendations, 2-116, 2-136
    results, 2-112
    scope, 2-53
    sources of, 2-10

T

V

W

Y